The Secret Language of Birds

TAROT

ADELE NOZEDAR & LINDA SUTTON

4880 Lower Valley Road • Atglen, PA 19310

All text by Adele Nozedar
All artwork by Linda Sutton

Copyright © 2011 Adele Nozedar and Linda Sutton

Library of Congress Control Number: 2011928578

All rights reserved. No part of this work may be reproduced or used in any form or by any means—graphic, electronic, or mechanical, including photocopying or information storage and retrieval systems—without written permission from the publisher.

The scanning, uploading and distribution of this book or any part thereof via the Internet or via any other means without the permission of the publisher is illegal and punishable by law. Please purchase only authorized editions and do not participate in or encourage the electronic piracy of copyrighted materials.

"Schiffer," "Schiffer Publishing Ltd. & Design," and the "Design of pen and ink well" are registered trademarks of Schiffer Publishing Ltd.

Designed by John P. Cheek
Type set in Trajan Pro/New Baskerville BT

ISBN: 978-0-7643-3900-4

Printed in China

Schiffer Books are available at special discounts for bulk purchases for sales promotions or premiums. Special editions, including personalized covers, corporate imprints, and excerpts can be created in large quantities for special needs. For more information contact the publisher:

Published by Schiffer Publishing Ltd.
4880 Lower Valley Road
Atglen, PA 19310
Phone: (610) 593-1777; Fax: (610) 593-2002
E-mail: Info@schifferbooks.com

For the largest selection of fine reference books on this and related subjects, please visit our website at
www.schifferbooks.com
We are always looking for people to write books on new and related subjects. If you have an idea for a book please contact us at the above address.

This book may be purchased from the publisher.
Include $5.00 for shipping.
Please try your bookstore first.
You may write for a free catalog.

In Europe, Schiffer books are distributed by
Bushwood Books
6 Marksbury Ave.
Kew Gardens
Surrey TW9 4JF England
Phone: 44 (0) 20 8392-8585; Fax: 44 (0) 20 8392-9876
E-mail: info@bushwoodbooks.co.uk
Website: www.bushwoodbooks.co.uk

DEDICATIONS

From Adele

For Oscar van Gelden, in memory of a promise. And for anyone who truly understands the value of a nice hedge, maybe even with a little brown bird sitting in it somewhere out of sight, singing.

From Linda

To my lovely father, Bill Sutton (1917-2006), who gave me a childhood of freedom and mental space, in which to create.

Acknowledgments

Thank You!

There have been many people who have helped along the way since I had the idea for *The Secret Language of Birds Tarot*. If I've left anyone out, profound apologies.

First, I'd like to thank the entire team at Harper Collins but in particular Wanda Whiteley, who took a flyer and gave me some incredibly invaluable advice a few years ago that resulted in Harper Collins publishing my first book, *The Secret Language of Birds*. This book had originally been intended as a Tarot deck so it's amazing that the idea has now come full circle.

Tarot reader, psychic and long-lost cousin Beryl Nozedar gave me place and a space to work on that original idea and for this I will always be grateful.

Philip and Stephanie Carr-Gomm have been incredibly encouraging and offered much practical advice and support. I'm also profoundly grateful to Philip for writing the foreword to this book.

The very lovely Barbara Moore, lover of all things to do with the Tarot, played a major part in making this deck happen.

Isabel Atherton of Creative Authors has been a huge help, as has James Duffett-Smith. I would also like to express my heartfelt thanks to Fiona Robertson who provided the illustrations for the tarot spreads.

Pete Schiffer and the entire Schiffer team have been wonderful to work with, and I'd particularly like to say a huge thank you to Dinah Roseberry who stayed late in her office on the day before Christmas Eve to email us with the news that the deck had been accepted; that was the best present that Linda and I could possibly have had.

The biggest thanks of all, from me, have to go to Linda Sutton. She immediately understood the idea of this Tarot and dedicated herself to producing some of the most beautiful paintings ever seen in any deck. She did this with no guarantee of publication or indeed with any idea whether these cards would see the light of day. The beauty, depth and subtlety of her paintings have gone way beyond anything I could ever have imagined. I feel very, very lucky to have her not only as a partner in this work but as a friend. Thank you, Linda, for making a dream come true.

Finally, both Linda and I owe a huge debt of gratitude to Dominic Di Chiera for his assiduous photography and help with this project.

Contents

Foreword by Philip Carr-Gomm 6

Introduction: The Winged Chariot 8

The Game of Gods & Birds: A Short History of the Tarot 14

The Twenty-Two Birds of the Major Arcana 16

The Four Flocks of the Minor Arcana (Cups, Wands, Swords, and Coins) 102

Divination with the Secret Language of Birds Tarot 202

Conclusion 208

FOREWORD BY PHILIP CARR-GOMM

A LITTLE BIRD TOLD ME...

    Intimations of how your life might turn out, of how you could grow and change, of how you could become the person you've always wanted to be, arrive in all sorts of ways: through half-remembered dreams, through the advice of a friend, the encouragement of a lover, the skilled guidance of a mentor. In almost every culture, though, such promptings and insights have also been sought in magical ways: through the images that might appear to a seer in a crystal ball or on the surface of a mirror, through the pattern made by falling earth on a drum-skin or sticks cast on the ground. But of all methods ever devised to see beyond appearances, to glimpse a deeper purpose, the Tarot is the most sophisticated.

    Whether this magical set of 78 cards originated in India or Egypt, or in the minds of Atlantean sages if they ever existed, we will never know. But we do know that the cards first appeared in the historical record in Italy in the fifteenth century, at that time of a great flowering of culture that gave birth not only to the most sophisticated system of divination, but also to that most sophisticated of art-forms: opera. And here in the glorious images of this Tarot the two combine, with the original Italian names for the Major Arcana, and half a dozen faces of famous singers to be discovered by opera lovers or the simply curious.

Anyone who has used the Tarot sensitively will know how it can speak to us. Here, though, we are introduced to a further dimension: We are invited to hear its song. In ancient times, sages and shamans, Daoists and Druids, indulged in ornithomancy: watching the flight and listening to the cries of birds to determine the wishes of the gods and the destiny of mortals. In this Tarot, the inspiration of this ancient art has been combined with modern understanding to offer something quite unique that calls to you from somewhere far away, which is at the same time very close: a realm of wisdom and of the heart, whose song sometimes sounds like the most haunting of operatic arias, sometimes like the most melodious birdsong, but which you know, deep down, to be in reality the song of your own soul, echoed back to you in the words you are reading and the images you are gazing upon.

Long may the beauty and the wisdom in this Tarot offer you guidance and inspiration!

~Philip Carr-Gomm
Author of *The DruidCraft Tarot*

Introduction
The Winged Chariot

*"How do you know
but every bird
that cuts the airy way
is an immense world of delight
closed to your senses five?"*

~William Blake
The Marriage of Heaven and Hell

Whilst writing the notes for this Tarot deck – which is the culmination of a seemingly idiotic idea that struck me like a bolt from the blue sometime back in 2004 – events were unfolding in my own life that, at the time, was taking increasingly bizarre (and some might say unreasonable) twists and turns than any seemingly random spread of a selection of 78 cards might possibly pre suppose.

But then, that's life.

We constantly try to analyze what's happening in our lives. We try to make sense of the senseless, often, and the time we need to process certain events can take years. We talk about "the benefit of hindsight" with good reason. And our ways of analysis change constantly.

When the earliest priests and Shaman discovered what they believed to be a link between the random vagaries of the weather and the actions of the Gods, they naturally turned toward the skies for confirmation and justification of their actions.

Birds, with their flight patterns and behavioral patterns, naturally assumed the nature of messengers from the lofty realms of these multitudinous Gods, since of course birds, symbolically, come from the same place as both Gods and weather; the vast, impenetrable Above. Our early deities automatically assumed all the many and varied characteristics of mankind, with a fair few hybridizations thrown in for good measure; the Gods could be kind or angry, malevolent of benevolent, patient and loving or quick to temper, mischievous, and all aspects beyond.

Dangerous deities were to be warned off, encouraged or appeased by the use of charms and talismans. Human enemies were cursed by invoking the same superhuman powers. Anything inexplicable remained mysterious, a rhyme and reason beyond the remit of a normal human being, forever the premise of our strange and terrible Gods.

BE CAREFUL WHAT YOU ASK FOR

If we could really define exactly what was going to happen in the future, what would this actually be like?

Imagine.

Every moment of true significance and every moment of inane mundanity mapped out, no surprises. Our lives would be effectively flatlined on a screen.

In truth, such an existence would be a living suicide mission – since we have to suppose we'd also know the exact time and nature of our own death – possibly the worse form of hell.

In truth, we can't predict the "future" with any great degree of accuracy. Anyone who boasts of such skills, or argues that it *is* possible, risks the accusation of being called at best deluded, or at worst, a liar.

So how, then, can it happen that you're reading such a statement here, in a book that accompanies a deck of tarot cards? Surely this is a contradiction in terms, given that the Tarot is surely meant to be a divinatory tool?

As ever, it's not that simple.

SMOKE AND MIRRORS

We need to look at things in a different way, to turn our opinions about such matters upside down, give them a good shake, turn them the right way up again and see what's there. We need to detach ourselves from the concept of linear time – or rather, from the idea of time as a linear entity.

If we can even just begin to understand this could be a possibility, then we are able to understand, and leave behind us, the realms of backward superstition and start to see the boundary lines where the known and explained (scientific) world meets that of the unknown and inexplicable (magical) one.

If we can do this, then we can conceptualize a place where there is not only no past and no future, but – and this is the hardest to grasp – no present either. That's a tricky one. After all, the present is defined by the past and the future... We need to try to change the parameters of the dimensions we have ourselves constructed. As there's no past and present, there's no death either. Interesting thought?

It can't be stated too strongly that in even wanting to have a look into a non-existent future, we start to tread on dangerous ground. We forget that we should only care about being in the moment of pure existence.

DON'T LOOK DOWN

It's only when we allow ourselves the dangerous luxury of stopping to take stock of what's going on and where we are that we take a real risk of shocking ourselves. If we are high up, then looking down can make us stumble. After all, we are not birds, and we can't fly.

The bird, naturally, knows no such fear of hesitation. Its ability to fly is the defining aspect that removes it from the remit of our normal human existence. Birds are as at home in the sky in the same way that fish are at home in the water, able to move freely and in any direction.

Human beings are designed in such a way that we are limited by our bodies. Our minds and intelligences, however, are unreigned and untrammeled.

The Mirage of Future Events

Our ancestors, as we've seen, looked to the skies for guidance from birds, their appearance, behavior, and flight patterns telling a rich story to the Augurs, who were adept in this secret language.

It's only commonsense for us to suppose that the birds that were the most prevalent were the birds that would have had the most to say. It's also commonsense to suppose that the sightings of rarer birds would also have had a significant part to play.

These same ancestors had a much closer relationship with the landscape, elements, and topography than we tend to do these days. Once, the weather could dictate the course of a battle, and a harvest made rotten by rain could literally mean life or death during times of knife-edge survival. Now, many of us are cocooned in our hermetically-sealed homes. And yet the weather – especially extremes of hot or cold – still plays a definitive part on how we have to lead our lives.

For these ancient people, the idea of looking into the future would have been looked upon as a folly, an unbridled luxury belonging to the realms of the effete. To them, the matter of day-to-day survival was all that mattered. At this level, then we can understand that the coming of certain birds at certain times of the year really *did* afford some reliable predictive measures. The cuckoo, for example, has always been heralded as the harbinger of summer. Greek fishermen made sure that their seasonal expeditions were heralded by the arrival of the swallows. Eventually, these practical avian indicators transformed themselves into more elaborate harbingers. Then the practice of augury really took flight. The augurs of Ancient Greece and Rome are relatively well-known, but you might not realize that every single society had similar practices, from Tibet to the Americas. Still, though, it's important to realize that there was no notion of gaining actual future knowledge via augury. The most that was asked was that the current course of events – seemingly decided upon by man – was ultimately in accord with the will of the Gods. In order to do this, the Augur-Priests devised quite elaborate methods of watching the birds – often blindfold, with the actions of the birds being carefully described so that the reading was as impartial as possible.

Free Will and Destiny

This practice, of making sure that the will of the Higher Beings was being carried out, presupposes a basic argument about free will versus destiny, always something of a dichotomy. There's the argument, put very simply, that the idea of "destiny" supposes that everything is preordained, i.e., decided prior to events. In this case, everything is meant to be part of a larger plan, a sort of game in which we are pawns. On the other hand, the idea of free will says that we are in fact masters of our own destiny, that we have it in our power not only to design our own futures, but that we can reconcile and reinstate ourselves with whatever has happened in the past. This can be painted as good, or bad, and depending on your own personal philosophy, either of these choices could be more or less valid.

However, there's also another way.

Nothing To Change But Your Own Mind

We can kick against the pricks, bemoan our fate, or see ourselves as somehow born under an "unlucky" star. All this is nonsense. With one fell swoop, we can alter all of this. The difficulty is in being able to rise above our petty everyday concerns and see the bigger picture. To gain clarity by seeing the birds' eye point of view, metaphorically speaking, of the entire arena of our lives, and in so doing, contextualize everything that happens to us – or indeed, everything that we *make* happen – in view of that bigger picture.

This is what's important: not to lose ourselves in a welter of detail, but to remember who we are and to remain true to ourselves, be in the moment, and to retain our own integrity. This is an ongoing process which we need to be reminded about from time to time. And this is where *The Secret Language of Birds Tarot* deck comes in.

The Tarot and Ornithomancy

Today, we might think that watching the flight patterns and behavior of birds in order to determine the outcome of certain events is a rather novel and fanciful idea. However, the provenance of this practice – known as "ornithomancy" – has a long history, and many illustrious characters have been involved with it. For example, think about St. Francis and his sermon to the birds. Or Apollonius of Tyana, who preceded Christ and seems to have shared many of the same talents: healing, raising people from the dead. Apollonius was reputed to speak the "language of the birds" as indeed was King Solomon, who, in a message from a bird was alerted about an incredibly beautiful and wealthy Queen: Sa'aba, or Sheba.

In ancient Greece the word for "omen" or "sign" was the same as that for "bird." Aristophane's play, *The Birds*, written in 414BC, tells of the birds that intercede between humankind and their Gods. And like Rome, founded by Romulus after signs from birds, Mexico City was founded at the spot decreed by legend, where an eagle would be seen perched upon a tree stump. These ancient tales underscore the profound symbolism carried by the bird, as a messenger from the Gods to mankind.

The Game of Birds & Gods

A Short History of the Tarot

You will notice that the deck you are holding contains a lot of Italian terminology. This is not only because the artist Linda Sutton lives for much of the time in Italy, but is also in honor of the origins of the Tarot cards as we now know them.

As Philip Carr-Gomm points out in his foreword, we are not certain of the exact origins of the Tarot, although there are many theories. Did they originate in Ancient Egypt? Do they contain Masonic references? Are they inextricably linked to the Kabbalah?

What we do know is that, as early as 1420, there are references to a certain "Game of Gods and Birds" which was commissioned by Duke Filippo Maria Visconti of Milan. The game, devised by Marziano da Tortona, was played with a deck of cards of four suits. Each suit represented "virtues, virginities, riches, and pleasures," and each suit was represented by a bird. These birds were eagles, phoenixes, turtledoves, and doves. And since this was all before the invention of the printing press, and each card had to be drawn and painted by hand, we must assume that decks of cards were a luxury item able to be enjoyed only by the very wealthy.

So whilst in fact this early deck wasn't the tarot deck as we know it today, it was an important forerunner. And so, in returning to the theme of birds in the *Secret Language of Birds Tarot*, our deck acknowledges another part of the early history of the Tarot.

Unlike latter-day Tarot cards, the very early Tarot decks were not used for divination, but for game-playing. One of the more prominent mentions we have of the cards being used for any other purpose comes in Cassanova's diary, when in 1765 he tells us that a mistress of his used such cards for fortune-telling, but it wasn't really until the circa nineteenth century that occultists became interested in the possibilities presented by the "Tarocchi." Today, of course, the Tarot is one of the major magical tools amongst psychics and occultists, and also has been acknowledged as a tool for psychoanalysis, particularly because of the work of Carl Jung.

The Twenty-Two Birds of the Major Arcana

The Spirit of the Tarot

When using the cards of the Major Arcana, think of the twenty-two cards as being one entity; try to imagine one spirit that unifies all the different images. During its journey, this spirit takes many forms, and despite the linear, numerical listing of all its aspects, the journey itself is certainly not a linear one, but one that moves backwards and forwards through time and space, and through the dimensions of experience, lessons learned, all the phases and waves of life.

0
THE FOOL

Il Matto
The Cuckoo

"He who has no fixed goal can never lose his way."

KEYWORDS
Innocent, free, spontaneous, careless, playful, optimistic, trusting.

DESCRIPTION
At the edge of a beach, pretty much where the sea meets the shore, we see a beguiling-looking young woman wearing a strapless gold sundress and a gold bangle. She's relaxed, looking over her shoulder in a come-hither manner, effectively flirting with the camera.

This girl looks as though she's more aware of her lipstick than of her surroundings – but the lipstick is good, and, in some cases, lipstick can be important especially when there might not be much else to rely on.

The bird that personifies the Fool is the cuckoo, and two cuckoos appear in this card. One flies up toward the woman and the other seems to be flying into the gaping jaws of the crocodile that occupies the foreground of the picture. The background of the painting is ambiguous; is it an island, or could it be a tsunami-like wave that's about to wash away the Fool and her companions?

THE FOOL AND THE CUCKOO

Like the Fool, the cuckoo seems to be able to break all the rules, and these are the rules that apply not only to the avian world, but to our world, too. The mother cuckoo behaves outrageously, laying her a single egg in the nest of another bird, effectively leaving a total stranger to nurture her child. The newly-hatched baby cuckoo is generally a monstrous size in comparison to its adopted siblings, eats ravenously, and can even eject the other birds from their own nest. What kind of stress must this cause for the surrogate mother, and would she ever suspect that she's been the subject of such a brazen hoodwink?

And why did the cuckoo itself adopt such radical behavior? Is she simply smarter than the average bird in ensuring decent hassle-free childcare, or is there a deep sadness that no cuckoo mother will ever enjoy seeing her child grow up? Is there something quite amoral in the way the cuckoo mother relies on the goodwill and responsibility – or perhaps sheer ignorance – of the selected surrogate mother?

SIGNIFICANCE OF THE FOOL AND THE CUCKOO

It's important to note the position of the fool in the pecking order of the Major Arcana. She's at the first position, with no real "number" at all, but stands at zero. Zero is a profoundly important little hula-hoop that can alter everything with its all-encompassing circular shape. It's as well to remember that the zero is the REAL magic circle, symbol of the Universe. Bear in mind, too, that in a standard deck of playing cards, the Fool has morphed itself the joker, the character that can upset the applecart wherever it appears. The Joker is able to be anything or nothing, can turn up at the start or end of the deck and can transform any other card it decides to stand next to; again, in mathematics, the zero has this same power.

Here, the Fool archetype is personified by the young girl, who is staring provocatively over her shoulder, seemingly oblivious to her surroundings; for example, she's dangerously close to both the ocean waves and the gaping jaw of the crocodile. In fact, if only she knew it, she's taking a gamble, and indeed the notion of risk and chance do belong to this card; that, and the carefree attitude of "here today, gone tomorrow" that some might see as foolhardy but which in fact can provide the greatest opportunities for learning, but only if we also take the attitude that there's no such thing as a mistake.

Why does the crocodile appear in such a weird landscape? Well, the Fool may weep tears, but not for long, and certainly not with any sense of remorse; they are the false tears of the crocodile. The sharpness of the crocodile's teeth is of no concern either to the Fool, who really doesn't give a damn about anything at all. This lady is content to soak up the sun wherever she is, trusting that the Universe will provide whatever she needs, whether this turns out to be luxurious surroundings and good fortune, or hard knocks and tough love.

An interesting aspect of this card is the dichotomy between destiny and free will. We might well take the view that every single thing we encounter could well be down to either of these concepts and that in reality it doesn't matter; what's important is how we choose to calibrate our thoughts. There's a saying that we can't change the world but we CAN change our minds, and the Fool is an apposite reminder of this.

This card is all about living in the moment and trusting to fate. The Fool can be infuriating to others, especially those who prefer their lives to have a plan, every moment accounted for. If you're such a person and have drawn this card, then it might be time to relax the rules a little and let your hair down.

Psychologists sometimes refer to the "inner child," the part of everyone that is able to take delight in small things and not worry about whatever tomorrow might bring. Whilst the concerns of everyday life do provide a necessary framework for many of us, sometimes a little spontaneity, doing something just for the hell of it and with no thought of financial remuneration can be a very good thing once in a while. None of us really knows if there's an afterlife, and it's best to live your live on the premise that we're a long time dead because then there's no "get out" clause. The Fool making an appearance here is all about the wisdom and beauty of living in the moment.

THE FOOL REVERSED

The Fool is unique amongst all the cards because it can go anywhere and any way up, and so it would be hypocritical to alter these rules for any reversal. Therefore, there's no need for any reversal summary here.

1
THE MAGICIAN

Il Bagatto

The Jay

"Me, I'm dishonest, and you can always trust a dishonest man to be dishonest. It's the honest ones you have to watch out for..."
~Johnny Depp

KEYWORDS
Magical powers, arcane knowledge, elemental forces, lateral thinking, inspiration, the trickster

DESCRIPTION
The Magician stares boldly back at us, challenging us to watch closely what he's doing. There are THREE of his birds, the jay, in the picture. He sits at a table, and on the table the

four elements that form the basis of the Minor Arcana appear as symbols. Above the head of the Magician floats the figure-of-eight, otherwise known as the lemniscate, that represents infinity. The opposing forces of Sun and Moon occupy the spaces in the loops.

The Magician is dressed in a formal-looking black jacket, but his shirt collar is casually open. This character is confident, certain, knows exactly what he's doing. On the lapels of the collar are the Alchemical symbol for quicksilver, and the astronomical map featuring the planet Mercury.

His hair has quite an unkempt appearance, fitting for his artistic and maverick temperament. He sits in front of a golden backdrop.

THE MAGICIAN AND THE JAY

The Jay, bursting suddenly through the forest foliage and just as unexpectedly disappearing again with a shriek and a figurative puff of smoke, is truly one of the most magical of birds. That flash of iridescent and transcendent blue, which leaves a streak of electricity across the darkness of the boughs, is constructed from the tiniest of feathers, each one intricately and perfectly colored and geometrically striped, the truly awe-inspiring work of a master craftsman. The mercurial appearance and disappearance of the jay is like an avian exclamation mark; it carries all the elements of surprise and astonishment of the most skilful sleight of hand. Like a magician's trick, there's smoke and mirrors here, and something else besides…

The jay is a member of the ultra-smart corvid family that also encompasses ravens, for example, and crows. Like these birds, jays can be good mimics of both musical instruments and the human voice; they indulge in a sort of auditory sleight-of-hand, if you will.

Because control over their territory is vitally important to the jay's particular kind of magic, the bird protects its own area fiercely. In the same way, here, the Magician is certainly master of the tools of his trade. And although when we observe the Magician at work we know that there's trickery involved, we are willing accomplices in his magic, happily complicit in our own deception.

This begs the question – who is deceiving who?

Significance of the Magician and the Jay

The Magician, above all else, signifies self-awareness, a combination of intellect and instinct working in conjunction with one another. In this he stands in contrast to the Fool, the drifter that works on blind intuition alone, hoping for the best. The array of elements, shown clearly in symbols on the table, show that The Magician is aware of his surroundings, understands the components of the Universe, and knows how to wield them to best effect. The Magician might show us the tools of his trade as though he has nothing to hide – but this transparency is all a part of his act.

The Magician, of course, has many tricks up his sleeve; but bear in mind that we, his audience, are willing accomplices in any sleight-of-hand or any play with smoke and mirrors. We are in the world, and of the world, and furthermore there's a belief in some circles that we have chosen everything in our lives. Whether or not this is your own personal philosophy, it can be quite a useful way of looking at things because then we really can become masters of our own destiny – just like The Magician.

Augurs used a staff to unite heaven and earth, and this Augur was in league with the "magician" or "great spirit" or "divinity" or whatever you want to call it, that sent the birds with their messages in the first place. Therefore, in this card we have the joining together of heaven and earth, male and female, light and dark, spirit and matter. What can't be understated, though, is something we've mentioned earlier; that is, the vital importance in the marrying together of instinct and intellect that this card is a reminder of. This is a powerful combination, the sort of union that enables us to think through all the aspects of a creative idea that are needed to make it manifest in the "real" world. It's as well to bear in mind that "creativity" is a state of mind rather than anything specifically to do with the arts. How you live your life, the choices you make, the work you do and the leisure time you enjoy are all processes of creative and conscious thought, as much the remit of the bookkeeper as the fine artist. Drawing this card could mean that you are on the brink of something that could change your life – it might not seem to be a big thing, but it could be a fundamental. You may have doubt or hesitation and you may be listening to too many of other peoples' opinions. Listen to yourself and have confidence that you, like the magician, can handle the elements that shape your destiny. Have no fear. Life is too short not to follow your dreams.

THE MAGICIAN REVERSED

We mentioned above that sometimes talking to too many people and listening to conflicting ideas – often from very well-meaning friends – can have a negative and confusing effect. However, sometimes we bottle things up to the extent that we internalize *so* much that we fill ourselves with self-doubt, and effectively block our lives and our energy by a process of prolonged indecision. It might be a good time to remove that block by talking to one select, impartial person. This might be a councilor, or a friend that is able to help you see a certain situation more clearly. If you draw this card as part of a reading, this help could well come from the reader sitting in front of you.

2
THE HIGH PRIESTESS

La Papessa

The Owl

"I am all that ever has been, all that is, and all that is to come, and no mortal has yet succeeded in lifting my veil."

KEYWORDS

Hidden depths, intuition, psychic powers, secrets, subconscious mind, wisdom, the occult

DESCRIPTION

It's a dark, a moon-lit night. The High Priestess, dressed in blue and surrounded by a flock of her birds, the owl, stands at the edge of a wood. Her position signifies her liminal

status – that is, a creature on the threshold of two worlds, this world and the Otherworld, one foot in each, able to span seen and unseen things, the conscious and the unconscious, knowledge and intuition. Here, the priestess is a young girl, her youth and beauty surprising given the wealth of knowledge that she holds; the High Priestess reminds us to expect the unexpected, since wisdom often comes to us in surprising ways. The Priestess holds a book in the folds of her dress – this volume, casually falling open but nevertheless with its information hidden, implies the secret knowledge and occult information that signifies the nature of both the Owl and the High Priestess; intuitive, reflective, mysterious; the female aspect.

THE HIGH PRIESTESS AND THE OWL

Its uniquely spooky appearance, mysterious nocturnal habits, and rare characteristics mean that the owl occupies a very special and important place in our collective consciousness, and has an equally unique symbolic significance that makes it the bird of the High Priestess. The Owl, like the High Priestess, is a nocturnal creature, and it's this nocturnal nature that has accorded both with access to hidden information and secret knowledge. Another physical aspect of the owl that gives a clue to its knowingness is the fact that its neck has 14 vertebrae – twice as many as in a human being – so the bird can swivel its head through 270 degrees; this bird, quite literally, can see behind itself. This is one of the reasons that the bird is associated with the hidden, the secretive, the occult. Our reverence for the owl – which has been on the planet for twenty-six million years – is such that it is one of the few birds to be featured in prehistoric cave paintings.

The Sumerian Goddess of Death, Lilith, was depicted in 2300BC as "winged, bird-footed, and accompanied by owls." Our ancestors believed that we accessed the gateway to the next world via the physical death of the body, and that certain creatures were able to act as "psychopomps," that is, they could guide us through this gateway. The owl had a very prominent position amongst these magical creatures. In Ancient Greece and Rome, the owl was associated with the Goddess of wisdom, Athena/Minerva.

Significance of the High Priestess and the Owl

The High Priestess is a mysterious, beautiful female figure. She carries a silence and stillness about her and emanates great strength. A.E. Waite makes the observation that "...there are some respects in which this card is the highest and holiest of the Major Arcana."

It has been said that the High Priestess, perhaps more than any other card, is representative of the person who is interpreting the cards.

But what does the card mean?

Put simply, the attributes of the High Priestess/owl are stillness, silence, wisdom, knowledge, and intuition, secrecy and mystery.

This attribute of power in silence and stillness also belongs to the owl; the feathers of the Owl have a structure which is different to that of other birds' feathers, which means that she makes no noise when she flies. The owl is a predatory bird, and the creatures which she takes as prey have no warning as to their fate. The High Priestess, like the Owl, has access to this world and the next, the world of the unrevealed. She carries that knowledge and can guide us towards what we need to know, and she will conceal what needs to be kept hidden, often for our own benefit.

It might well be that this is a time to be still, to be silent, and to trust in the knowledge that all is well with the universe. Although some of us may see "keeping still" as a passive activity to be frowned on, we have to find a balance between action and reflection.

It's possible that you want to take time out from your everyday life, to rediscover your path. This decision – to stop what you are doing and simply see what happens next – requires great courage and fortitude, and is a decision not taken lightly. It might help for you to go out into the places inhabited by owls, the bosky green woods at the time of twilight, and meditate, to find the stillness inside that provides such an immense core of power.

The "shape shifting" ability of the High Priestess is a quality shared by the moon, which changes through every day of its twenty-eight-day cycle. This is a reminder that the High Priestess may not be what she appears to be. This is why in this card the priestess appears as a young girl, her age belying her wisdom. Secrets are generally revealed in quite oblique ways; this is a mark of the High Priestess at work. Bear in mind that the Owl has access to information which is usually concealed during the hours of darkness, so pay attention to your dreams or sudden flashes of intuition.

THE HIGH PRIESTESS REVERSED

A reversal of the High Priestess/owl card is an indicator of the need to find balance in all aspects of life; dark and light, happy and sad. Sometimes, when we go through phases of contemplation, it can be easy to retreat too far into the internal world, and it's as well to be aware of the need to keep a balance between that inner, spiritual world and the external, material one. Similarly, you need to recognize the time for action as you recognize the time for stillness. Pay objective attention to the inner voice and be aware that sometimes you can be guilty of wishful thinking; that is, ignoring your intuition in favour of what you desire. Trust that inner voice.

3
THE EMPRESS

L'Imperatrice
The Dove

"There never was a woman like her...she was gentle as a dove and brave as a lioness."
~US President Andrew Jackson speaking about his mother

KEYWORDS

The Mother, fertility, abundance, love, beauty, healing powers, kindness, inspiration

DESCRIPTION

Against a sky-blue background, the Empress poses enticingly, one arm reaching up to the Heavens, the other pointing to the Earth. She wears a circlet of seven stars, which represent the seven stars of the Pleides, also called the Seven Doves. The dove is the bird that personifies the Empress in her aspect as the Great Mother, and there are three doves depicted here. One hovers above her shoulder, the second hovers at hip level, and the third appears in the gold patterns of her dress. Tattooed on the Empress' arm is a globe, surmounted by a cross, also known as the Globus Cruciger, which is one of the early symbols of Christian dominion over the Earth. Inevitably, there's a more elaborate and all-encompassing explanation of such a sign.

THE EMPRESS AND THE DOVE

The Empress represents the higher aspect of feminine energy – the Madonna, the Earth Mother, all those gentle and compassionate energies. In relation to this, appropriately enough, the Dove shares exactly the same meaning, without exception, all over the World from America where it counterbalances the hawk, to Mecca, where they enjoy sacred status as a bird specially favored by Mohammed. However, as well as this nurturing aspect, the dove – and its close cousin the pigeon – symbolize not only motherhood, but also fertility, purely because of their ability to procreate prolifically. The soft, soothing, and mellow cooing of doves sounds similar to the crooning of mothers to their babies. Aphrodite/Venus, the personification of The Empress in Greek/Roman myth, also has the dove as her familiar. It's doves that fed and nurtured the infant Zeus when he was helplessly hidden in a cave.

We have to look beyond the political imagery appropriated by religions, and observe their iconic images to understand what's really happening. The Madonna is the personification of The Goddess for the Catholic Church, and again, it's common currency to see her with the white dove that represents the Holy Spirit. Why should it be this bird above all others that takes on this role in such popular and meaningful religious iconography? Well, think of the humble carrier pigeon. We might think these days that they're just the hobby of certain old folk, but it's a fact that these birds have a far more illustrious history. For example, in the *Bible* it was the dove that returned to Noah, bearing the sprig of green in its beak, as a message that the ark was close to dry land. This is perhaps one of the most notable examples of Holy Spirit appearing in the guise of any bird. The navigational skills of these birds is prodigious, arguably the best amongst in all the avian kingdom. To give you an idea, a pigeon can fly up to 600 miles without a break – and they can do it fast. These skills have proved more vital in past times than perhaps they do today; for example, during the early Olympic Games, it was pigeons that carried the news of team victories by the method of colored ribbons tied around their legs. Napoleon's defeat at Waterloo was announced by pigeons sent by the Rothschild family. And during both World Wars, pigeons had a crucial part to play. One, called Snow White, was even awarded the illustrious Military Cross in recognition of her service. The German forces took control of over a million Belgian racing pigeons, and there's a memorial in Lille to the 20,000+ birds that we know for certain lost their lives during this time – another nod to the sacrifice made to the greater good by The Madonna herself.

In Ancient Greece there was a magical forest – a real place, not a myth – where a dove perched in the branches of a sacred oak. This dove was said to have oracular powers, and the priestesses there were known as "doves" in its honor.

SIGNIFICANCE OF THE EMPRESS AND THE DOVE

Passion, sensuality, nurturing, the sacrifice of the self, in essence, to creative ideas is the message carried by this card. And it's as well to remember that this card is not just about giving birth to children, or motherhood in its most obvious form. The process of gestation applies not only to giving birth to a child, but also to an idea. An idea, just like a child, can be all-absorbing, all-encompassing. However, sometimes we feel guilty about giving in to these creative ideas, worried that they might interfere with "real" life. Give in to this urge and relax, put away any stresses, and realize that whatever is happening in your life will be ultimately fulfilling despite any qualms or fears you might have. This fear comes from the deep-rooted seat of the ego, which often does anything it can to keep the status quo and avoid change.

As the Earth Mother, The Empress reminds us to take pleasure in the smallest of things, the tiny miracles of nature that might seem insignificant but which are overwhelmingly beautiful.

When we are inspired with a creative idea, it's as though we are driven forward by a power that seems as though it's outside our control. Such inspiration is the basis behind the spark that is sometimes called "divine." This is the same force that made St. Teresa of Avila believe that she could fly. The Empress can appear as this Muse, and you may find that your life will be very different in some months hence. Because of the maternal and nurturing aspects of the Dove, any changes that need to be made will take place gently and naturally, their effects fully absorbed to bring you to the exact place that you need to be in your life. During all this, it's essential that you pay attention to, and take care of, your own needs; otherwise you won't be able to do the same for others.

Another aspect of the Dove/Goddess is the need to trust. Sometimes events in our lives make us wary, and often with very good reason. If there's anything you're unsure about – particularly in relation to a new love or a new idea or project – have faith in your feelings and go with the flow. If in any doubt, try asking The Empress for a sign to show you the way. Synchronicity operates all the time, but we go through phases of being either more or less receptive to it.

THE EMPRESS REVERSED

If this card appears upside down in the spread, on first glance it might appear that perhaps there are problems with your own "fertility," whether in the usual physical sense of the word or in terms of creative outlets. Sometimes when we have blockages in any area we need to take a good hard look at what might be causing them; perhaps for some reason you've turned away from the sexual, sensual side of life, which can affect our happiness and productivity? Perhaps you have been neglecting yourself, forgetting to take care of the most important person in your life. Taking care of yourself isn't an act of selfishness, but of selflessness. Drawn reversed, too, this card can indicate poverty. However, what *is* poverty? Is it a simple lack of financial means, or is it a poverty of the spirit? You might find yourself surrounded by expensive material goods, however, it might be time to take a look at what in your life is truly meaningful, and start to prioritize that above anything else.

4
THE EMPEROR

L'Imperatore

The Hawk

"In the practise of tolerance, one's enemy is the best teacher."
    ~His Holiness, the Dalai Lama

KEYWORDS

The Father, stability, protection, wealth, authority, leadership, power, discipline, restriction

DESCRIPTION

Against a blue sky, The Emperor stands. His body language is bold, regal, haughty. There's no doubt from his clothing and body language that HE is in control, HE is in charge, HE is the man that everybody else answers to. He's dressed

in the red that represents the power of a royal blood line, and the gold that speaks of wealth. One hand is casually tucked into his belt, master of all he surveys. Two of the hawks that are the avian representatives of The Emperor are shown here; one, he is in control of, the bird grasped firmly in his left hand. The other flies free but stays close, and even the all-powerful Emperor is looking towards the bird as if for direction and guidance.

The Emperor displays two symbols to further underline his character. On his breast appears the Maltese Cross surmounted by a crescent moon, and on his belt appears the five-pointed star and another crescent moon. These symbols tell us that The Emperor is aligned to the patriarchal religions.

THE EMPEROR AND THE HAWK

As The Empress/Dove represents all aspects of feminine power and grace, The Emperor/Hawk is her opposite number. In the American House of Congress, the Doves and the Hawks similarly oppose one another. We still speak frequently of the Earth Mother, and once we spoke as frequently of the Sky Father. Maybe we should revive the term, especially with regard to The Emperor, because this is what he is. The Sky Father.

In Ancient Egypt, the hawk – or falcon, for that matter – came to stand as the symbol for a God, a masculine, paternal dictator that could be benevolent but also wrathful – very much the aspect of any patriarch. In particular, this hawk-headed God was Horus, the God of the Sky, who shaded and protected the Earth with his outstretched wings. It was believed that one of his eyes was the Sun, and the other, the Moon. The Sun God, Re, also appears as the Hawk, as does the God of War who bears the same characteristics as the Greek Apollo.

So here in the Hawk we have the personification of male energies, both positive and negative. The Emperor is a distinctly mature figure, full of authority and worldliness, wearing the sort of clothes that are in keeping with his status.

The Significance of the Emperor and the Hawk

We use the term "hawk eyed" to mean someone who misses nothing, whose eyesight is incredibly keen. Similarly, to "watch someone like a hawk" refers to the utter focus and concentration that a hawk gives to its prey. This predatory nature is also one of the qualities of The Emperor. And again like the hawk, The Emperor is very keen to assert his dominance over his territory by chasing off invaders.

Male energies alone, however, are as imbalanced as those of solely female energies. We need both to provide real harmony. It's no coincidence that the number four belongs to this card; the primary significance of this number is "stability." Think of the four legs of a table, or the four walls of a house. We need the one, two, and three to get to the four, after all. True stability is a question of the harmony of opposing forces; sun and moon, light and dark, hard and soft. Even the hunter and the hunted, the hawk and his prey, strike a balance within nature that makes sense to both parties, defines their roles.

All the instinct and feminine intuition of The Empress are countered here by control and a rather rigid way of thinking. Literally empirical, The Emperor likes to weigh and measure things, and there is little room for metaphysics in his life. These qualities, along with the strict rules and boundaries that are his remit, can make The Emperor often seem a restrictive power. However, restrictions help us to define our lives, to decide what's acceptable and what isn't. The Emperor has high moral values but must be careful that these values don't come across as intolerance.

Clarity of thought and immediacy of action are the remit of The Emperor, both valuable assets. The Emperor speaks the truth, which you can recognize immediately by the timbre of his voice. He is secure, knowledgeable, master of all he surveys – which he does, often, with that hawk-like gaze. Any male figure of authority, in real life, can represent The Emperor. As well as a father, the Emperor could be a powerful employer, a disciplinarian teacher, a patriarch or patron, or even some sort of official body that shares those same values. The Emperor might sometimes be referred to as a control freak, however, boundaries can define ethical rights and wrongs just as well as territorial borders.

THE EMPEROR REVERSED

There's more to life than those things that can be weighed or measured. The world of the imagination is equally valid; many great scientific discoveries are triggered by seemingly random events that inspire a spark of lateral thought – Newton being hit on the head with an apple, for example. The rigid discipline and control favored by The Emperor means that he can sometimes miss things that are right under his nose. Be aware that, whilst rational thought is a prerequisite for The Emperor, there needs to be tolerance for those whose minds work in a different way. There's a thin dividing line between the tolerant disciplinarian and the despotic tyrant. It's easy for The Emperor to crush those around him with criticism, easy for that clear voice to be raised in anger. And it can also be easy for that anger to be misinterpreted, causing those surrounding The Emperor to be afraid. Rules, after all, are made to be broken. Snap them in two occasionally.

5
THE HIGH PRIEST

Il Papa

The Kite

"Art is not a pastime, but a priesthood."
~Jean Cocteau

KEYWORDS
Authority, religion, education, quest for knowledge, counsel, initiation, concord

DESCRIPTION
The High Priest stands against a dramatic background of greeny-blue and gold. He appears jubilant and confident and is smiling, his arms outstretched as if he's embracing the World. The bird that represents this character is the kite, and there are three depicted here. One perches on his left hand. The other flies above

his head. And a third appears in silhouette, circling high up in the sky.

A multitude of symbols appear on the card. On the left-hand lapel of The High Priest's jacket is the astrological symbol for Libra, and on the right are the crossed keys, symbol of The Vatican State and a nod to Il Papa, The Pope. Also appearing running down the right hand side are the astrological symbols for Taurus, Scorpio, Leo, and Aquarius. These last four personify Earth, Water, Fire, and Air.

THE HIGH PRIEST AND THE KITE

Kites are found all over the world, although in some places their numbers are dropping. Since The High Priest can represent the father-figure priest of the old patriarchal faiths, the drop in numbers of the birds could also mirror the turning away from these beliefs.

Kites make a distinctive shape in the sky, their large wingspan and pointed tails almost giving the silhouette of a giant swallow. Like the swallow, in Ancient Greece the Kite was so well respected when it appeared to mark the beginning of spring, that people would bow to it in the same way that they gave obeisance to their priests. Others might even grovel or turn somersaults! Another Greek myth tells that the kite was once a King whose indiscretions resulted in him being transformed into a bird.

Augurs believed that kites had powers of clairvoyance. Bear in mind that this word means "clear sight," a power that we associate with the rational thought processes of a priest. This priestly aspect is also reflected in an Egyptian myth, which tells that the first book of religious laws and customs was brought by the kite to Thebes. In this instance, the bird was carrying these rules and instructions directly from the Gods themselves – again, the role of the Priest. In India, the Brahminy Kite is the sacred bird of the priestly caste of the Brahmins, as its name suggests.

SIGNIFICANCE OF THE HIGH PRIEST AND THE KITE

Of course, the High Priest is the male counterpart of The High Priestess. Whereas she is nocturnal and secretive, associated with occult powers, The High Priest is the opposite; he is overt, often mainstream. If The High Priestess signifies all the powers of the "alternative" spiritualities, The High Priest stands for the order and traditions of the established patriarchal religions – Christianity, Judaism, Islam.

The High Priest is also something of a political character, since the Church and The Law are inextricably linked. In that marriage can often be a political act, The High Priest is a reminder of the idea of marriage – in whatever form it takes. Sometimes we find ourselves in a "marriage" which may be one of convenience, rather than emotion. A partnership is a sort of marriage. And bear in mind that a true marriage is an exchange of ideals, emotions, needs, and wants to mutual advantage. Sometimes one partner may take the lead, sometimes the other will do so. The High Priest understands the core of what a true marriage really is.

The High Priest represents a figure of authority, not just in the religious sphere. He could be a teacher, a counselor, and kind of guiding figure. He could even be the guide that you encounter on a mountaineering trip! He is someone that is able to give assistance whilst allowing someone to use their own intuitive powers. Unlike The Emperor, The High Priest is not a control freak!

THE HIGH PRIEST REVERSED

In that the High Priest can indicate the regulation and order of organized religion and the power of a group, when reversed, this card speaks of anarchy and the responsibility of the individual to him or herself alone. Of course, what's good for one person is generally good for the society as a whole, but there's a tendency for some free-thinkers, particularly youthful and inexperienced ones, to act in an incendiary manner to put their point across. The High Priest, reversed, is the card of the protester, the anarchist, and the revolutionary. Be careful to temper this anarchistic passion with commonsense and a careful use of the sort of language which will unite rather than divide.

6
THE LOVERS

Gli Amanti

The Parrot

"We waste time looking for the perfect lover, instead of creating the perfect love."
~Tom Robbins

KEYWORDS
Beauty, sensuality, attraction, youth, yearning, union, harmony, obsession, infatuation

DESCRIPTION
Against a sky-blue background The Lovers embrace. Their body language speaks of sensual yearning; a melding and melting of bodies. He is bare-chested, wears jeans. She wears a shimmering golden shirt, a gold hoop earring, and a golden bangle. He leans toward her, she throws her head

back in abandon. Both have their eyes shut as if to concentrate more fully on the overtly sensual, physical aspect of their pose. There is no eye contact. The bird that signifies The Lovers is the parrot, and there are two colorful members of the variety here. One is perched on his shoulder, and the other is perched on her wrist, seemingly hanging onto the bangle.

THE LOVERS AND THE PARROT

Why should the parrot be associated with the Lovers? The original inspiration for the connection comes from India. There, the bird is dedicated to the God of Love, Kama. We talk about "parrot fashion," meaning to repeat what someone says as part of a way of learning, or to imitate someone. When people fall in love they tend to mimic one another; they mirror each others' body language, their way of laughing, and often their way of speaking. One partner might even decide that certain habits that they might have previously eschewed – such as smoking – are acceptable in the other. The smell of the smoke might even start to be appealing purely because it is connected with the person. Because of all these reasons, the bird is a symbol of marriage in India – another fact that accords the parrot sacred status as a bird of love.

Parrots are beautiful, affectionate, and we do love them because of their often human-seeming traits. Although parrots that have been taught to speak often say things seemingly at random, sometimes they say things that are uncannily appropriate. The beauty of the parrot, too, is attractively dazzling, and sometimes belies the bad temper and anti-social habits of the bird. Beware, love can be blind!

THE SIGNIFICANCE OF THE LOVERS AND THE PARROT

As we've seen, when people first fall in love they mirror one another in many ways, and this is right and natural in those heady initial stages. But is this absolutely honest? Okay, we might move or shift our ideas slightly to accommodate someone who we are interested in, but if we're not careful, it can sometimes happen that the "weaker" of the two partners can end up by subsuming him or herself, losing identity in the process. And then the other partner will turn around at some point and wonder what it was he or she fell in love with in the first place. So when we talk about The Lovers, it's as well to remember that true love means being yourself, first and foremost, and remembering who you are. You might notice that these lovers have their eyes closed – they're involved in the realm of the senses and the emotions, not the intellect. They're not making eye contact.

In drawing this card, often the first reaction is one of excitement and anticipation. But the card doesn't carry a simple tale of *loveydoveyness*, not by a long chalk. It's more complex than that. There's the matter of choice, and the part played by the rational mind as well as the human instinct to procreate. What's left after the first heady rush of physical passion? Is there enough to build on, to turn attraction into something more deep and meaningful, and to create that perfect love?

This card is a reminder to hold out for the fully-rounded kind of love that has meaning beyond those initial stages of sexual desire and passion. Although desire and passion might form the basis for a long relationship, we can be effectively blinded by them and may "wake up" after the fireworks have fizzled out to find that there is very little else that we have in common. The process of "falling in love" might be more or less at first sight, but this card is all about looking beyond the forest fire of a powerful initial attraction.

THE LOVERS REVERSED

If The Lovers card appears reversed in a spread, it can indicate the unhealthy aspects of emotions that might appear to be love, but which are not. This includes obsessive behavior, unreasonable jealousy, the use of sex as a means of control. It speaks of choices made for the wrong reasons – the calculating choice made because of wealth or status rather than true love, or a relationship born of convenience. Sometimes when we're lonely we get together with someone to alleviate that feeling. It's as well to remember that unless you are whole, complete, and satisfied in your own skin, it's unfair to expect a partnership to "mend" you. It's easy, if we are insecure, to get "locked in" to a relationship that can be abusive and disabling. Look closely to make sure that this isn't happening to you.

7
THE CHARIOT

Il Carro
The Eagle

"Know thyself to be sitting in the chariot, the body to be the chariot, the intellect the charioteer, and the mind the reins."
~Veda Upanishads, 800BC

KEYWORDS
A journey, fortune, war, triumph, ego, fame, success, mastery, the will, determination, long-sightedness

DESCRIPTION
Against a golden and verdigris background, The Chariot emerges. Astride it is a beautiful naked woman with long, loose black hair and a golden circlet. We realize that the Chariot

Major Arcana 43

itself is represented by two eagles, the bird that personifies this card, which also traditionally belongs to the astrological sign of Leo. The Eagles are white, which stands for purity.

The woman carries a staff-like object which could either be a riding crop or a wand. It's surmounted by the wings – symbolizing spiritual realization – and the five pointed star that has a multitude of meanings, including knowledge and mankind.

There's also a posy of two flowers between the heads of the two eagles. The flowers signify youthful exuberance and beauty.

THE CHARIOT AND THE EAGLE

The mythos of the eagle is one of the richest and most varied of the entire bird world, the symbolic meanings of power, force, and authority the same the world over. The bird's power and special qualities mean that it has long been associated with empires and majesty. The eagle carried thunderbolts for Zeus, indicated the site of the Omphalos in Delphi, and was one of the most auspicious birds in any practice of augury. The eyesight of the eagle, in particular, is a quality that's often singled out; we all know what "eagle eyed" means. There's a physical reality behind this saying, too. The bird has a sort of telescopic vision that enables it to scan a terrain of three square miles when soaring at a height of one thousand meters, and any prey attacked by the bird wouldn't have any idea what hit it. The word "acumen," meaning "precision," comes from the Latin for *Eagle*, "aquilus." The soaring, effortless flight of the eagle means that it's the bird most associated with solar powers, and is legendarily believed to be able to look at the Sun itself with no adverse effects. The golden color of the eagle is of the Sun, too, a shared brilliance, one reflecting the other.

The Chariot is the card of willpower, mastery, the "long vision" and the bigger picture. It's also the card that indicates the parallel streams of consciousness and destiny. That is, the state in which we have full awareness that everything we do, even the smallest of actions, is part of the great web of wholeness that forms the Universe. We can understand this as a theory, perhaps, but true experience of that understanding is a rare privilege. Anyone who has this experience will find that their life changes as a result.

The Significance of the Eagle and the Chariot

Why are we here? What is our purpose in life? What's it all about? Notice that The Chariot is making forward progress but that the woman who is mounted behind the eagles is pretty relaxed about the whole thing. She is not "driving" the chariot, nor is she allowing herself to be driven. She is at one with her own vehicle, relaxed enough to be naked and proud of it, and a reminder of the idea that our own destiny is always tied into the bigger picture, the greater universe. This may not be your personal philosophy, but chances are that if you are delving into the metaphysical associations of the tarot, then you will have enough of an open mind to accept this as a possibility. The two eagles here represent the intellect and intuition, the conscious and the subconscious, matter and spirit. This is the dream of being naked in a crowd and then realizing that it doesn't matter, that you have nothing to hide. It's the reality of knowing that everything is exactly as it should be, that all is well and is happening according to divine will – which is of course the true meaning of the word "divination." A tarot reading is all about reminding us of the continuous connection with the moment, the "now." The "now" that we are always a part of, whether or not we are always fully conscious of it.

This awareness gives us a razor-sharp precision, makes us "eagle-eyed" in terms of our conscious awareness. But attaining such a rarefied talent is not always easy, and it's likely that it could be the result of a baptism of fire. Jung called this process "individuation," a state sometimes brought about by great trauma due to events that were awful at the time, but which result in enlightenment and a heightened awareness. For example, sobriety after drug addiction or alcoholism is more profound purely because of the contrast of experience. Happiness is more profound after grief. We only realize that death has no meaning when we are brought face to face with it. All these experiences serve to give us a greater connection to our own lives and a realization that, in the same way that the beautiful woman is a part of the chariot rather than just the driver, we are our own vehicle, driver, and destination, all in one. Like the eagle, we are powerful, secure, liberated; this card shows us that difficulties can be mastered and that there's no such thing as misfortune. There's no need to fight, because there's nothing to resist. Paradoxically, when Christ told us to offer the other cheek, he did so in the spirit of The Chariot. The sureness of total power makes us kind and compassionate.

THE CHARIOT REVERSED

Any symbol which is particularly powerful – such as that of the Chariot or the eagle – is more liable to have that power turned upon itself in a negative way, simply because there's more power to be turned! For example, totalitarian regimes – such as Nazi Germany or the Roman Empire – adopted the eagle as a symbol of their might, despite the corruption of these regimes. As a result, the symbol itself became associated with all the worst qualities of absolute power – fascism, rigid control, humourlessness, cruelty. It's as well to ensure that those parallel streams of intuition and intellect are working in harmony, since a balance in favor of either can upset the smooth running of the chariot. It's time to examine your motives and ensure that your objectives are honest. Then your course of action will run smooth.

8
STRENGTH

La Forza

The Hummingbird

"Out of the eater came forth meat, and out of the strong came forth sweetness."
~Judges 14:14

KEYWORDS

Energy, action, power, courage, generosity, confidence, charisma, mind over matter

DESCRIPTION

A beautiful woman, with long black hair and colorfully dressed in a red dress, a pink skirt, and a purple belt, lounges casually against a golden disc, which could be a halo or could be the Sun. Leaning against her, looking at her adoringly, is a lion, his gaze fixed raptly

on her face, jaws apart in a relaxed manner as though he's smiling at the woman. The bird that represents the idea of strength is the hummingbird, and two of them are depicted here. One hovers above the head of the lion, and the other is flying over the head of the woman, crossing the part where the golden disc meets the blue of the sky.

STRENGTH AND THE HUMMINGBIRD

Why would such a tiny bird be used here to represent the idea of strength?

Well, size isn't everything, and strength isn't all about brute force. In the tarot, as in life, it's a far more subtle quality. The specific story that links the smallest of birds to one of the more powerful concepts comes from the Americas – not surprising given that here, the hummingbird distribution is high. The greatest Aztec God, Huitzilpochtli, the most powerful warrior of all, appears in the form of a hummingbird. This name means "hummingbird that comes from the left," with "left" in this instance referring to the world of Spirit. The Aztecs also believed that tiny hummingbirds turned into soldiers at night in order to do battle with the powers of darkness.

A giant hummingbird – which can be seen in its full glory only when viewed from the air, and so would never have been seen properly by the people that created it – appears on the Nazca Plains in Peru. The effort that must have gone into making such an image is a good indicator of the reverence in which the bird was held.

Hummingbirds have a truly remarkable aerial dexterity. They can hover vertically or horizontally, can move backwards and forwards. Their wings beat at between fifty and seventy-five times per second, and as they do so, they make the distinctive humming sound that gives the bird its name.

The hummingbird lives on the nectar of flowers, made from sunshine; in fact, the bird plays a major part in actually pollinating the flowers. In Brazil, the bird is called the "flower kisser."

Significance of Strength and the Hummingbird

There are certain branches of martial arts, such as Wing Chun (legendarily "invented" by an oriental nun in order to repel the advances of men), which takes someone else's power and energy and, with deft movements that require little physical force, is able to turn that energy back on itself and render the would-be attacker harmless. This is one aspect of the sort of strength we're talking about with the hummingbird card. Here, the fragile femininity of the girl in red sits comfortably with the powerful lion, who is rendered kitten-like rather than ferocious. Patience is a sort of strength, too; think of the quiet plodding and industry required by bees gathering the materials to make their hive, itself a sturdy and miraculous honeycomb construction which not only provides a home for the colony but a place to store honey, that is gathered with an equal amount of patience. Did you know that it takes one bee its entire lifetime to make just one teaspoonful of honey? Any disciplined practice, such as yoga, meditation or even writing a book, makes for an empowering end result that is way more than the sum of the parts or the little drips of time that contribute to the end result. Those Indians who decided to etch the gigantic hummingbird on the Nazca plains are a good example of such tenacity.

The Strength card is also about marriage of sorts, the union of opposites; yin and yang, of course, but something that's a little bit more than that. A true union of man and woman makes each of them "more;" the woman more feminine, and the man more manly. This is the card of the attraction of opposites; the caveman and the princess. This might be a brief relationship since such extreme opposites may be hard to sustain, but is nevertheless a once-in-a-lifetime opportunity to experience something truly transformative and ecstatic. In order to achieve such a result, there's a certain amount of surrender required – again, it requires strength, and security, to willingly relinquish control so as to allow the other person in. What happens next will depend on the intellectual rigor of both parties. Very often, such a balance of power can have a see-saw effect until both find out how to live in harmony, each giving and taking equally, sweetness and strength equal parts.

STRENGTH REVERSED

Where there are equal powers, either in one person or in a partnership, these energies can sometimes come into conflict. For example, someone who is very masculine, someone who displays the powers attributed to the Emperor, perhaps, might be fatherly, but might display despotic traits too. And someone who is tender and giving, qualities associated with femininity, might also seem to be insipid or weak. Beyond the initial attraction, opposing types might find that they have insoluble differences which can weaken both parties by emphasizing the worst aspects of both. Abuser and abused, for example, stray into this category. We need to find personal balance by unifying any conflicting traits. In order to do this, however, we need to understand, quite clinically, what these traits are. This is where a good friend can show their true worth by pointing out those qualities that could be improved on. It might not be comfortable to hear some of what they have to say, but it's essential to listen if we're to develop into fully functioning, adult human beings.

9
THE HERMIT

L'Eremita
The Peregrine Falcon

"The hermit doesn't sleep at night, in love with the blue of a vacant moon; the cool of the breeze that rustles the trees rustles him too."

~Anon

KEYWORDS
Meditation, solitude, self-reliance, ingenuity, knowledge, self-denial, circumspection, withdrawal

DESCRIPTION
Against a gold and verdigris background, a young woman sits, her back to us, glancing at us over her right shoulder. She has a sultry manner

but isn't really paying a great deal of attention to whoever might be watching. The woman is clad in a backless white dress and she's wearing a daisy chain thrown casually around her neck, back to front, therefore visible to the observer. She's sitting on the grass, and behind her is a book with a blue cover that shows a red question mark on the front.

The bird that represents the personification of The Hermit is the peregrine falcon. Three of the birds are depicted here; one perches on the woman's leg and looks down toward the ground, the other perches on her shoulder and looks toward us, and a third flies close to her head, wings outstretched.

The Hermit and the Peregrine Falcon

The Peregrine is believed to be one of the fastest creatures on earth; it's been recorded flying from a plane, chasing a piece of meat thrown by the pilot, at over two hundred and twenty miles per hour. The bird in question was probably flying even faster than this, but the recorded speed was the absolute limit of the equipment that was available at the time. Now, high velocity might not be the most immediate association with the hermit, but there is a connection in that speed that is a unique factor of this card. The definition here is that the peregrine flies at its own speed, a talent unavailable to other creatures. Fast or slow doesn't really matter. It is the fact that the hermit chooses her own pace that matters. Others might find this difficult to live with or to understand.

The peregrine is also extremely predatory, and is coldly efficient with that prey. A racing pigeon, efficiently despatched by the peregrine diving down on it from above, doesn't know what hits it and feels no pain as it is killed. This predatory nature can also be a quality of the hermit archetype. Choosing not to socialize since there are few of her kind, nevertheless there are certain things that can only be provided for The Hermit by another person. The Hermit is adept at selecting these necessities – and people – without ever really entering the real-life infrastructure of society at large.

Like the peregrine that chooses not to build its own nest but to tidy up the vacant nests left by other birds, The Hermit is extremely ingenious. The lack of financial resources that seem to be part of The Hermit's remit means that she is adept at fixing things, making something out of nothing, and using leftovers.

The Significance of The Hermit and the Peregrine Falcon

In many interpretations of this card, the emphasis often falls on the meditative aspects of solitude, and the need to spend some time alone in order for a certain spiritual aspect of the self to be realized. Whilst all this is true, it's also often apparent that the real nature of the life of a hermit also has to be about making a real connection with the actual world, the planet earth itself. It's other people that The Hermit removes him or herself from. There might be a multitude of reasons for this, but whatever it is, the effects of such a withdrawal from normal human society can be that The Hermit notices the natural world far more acutely and has an empathy for it that may not extend to his or her own kind. The Hermit often has such a thin skin, and can be so sensitive, that the normal habits of other people can jar and seem offensive – in particular, the infrastructure of "normal" everyday life such as electronics, screens, mobile phones, and internet technology. All this paraphernalia can be alarming. Although these ways of communication undoubtedly have their benefits, they can also provide a useful means for people to avoid real connection.

To embark on a solitary life requires determination, focus, and a strength of will that is often hard-won, and The Hermit may have spent many years achieving the steely determination that gives her the courage to embark on such a rigorous spiritual quest. Both the peregrine and The Hermit choose to inhabit places that are lone and inaccessible.

THE HERMIT REVERSED

The Hermit is an uncompromising character. Faced with the eddies and currents of the everyday life of simpler people, The Hermit sees conflict and nonsense. It's as well to remember that when we live alone, we often get into habits that we don't realize we have, and which we carry on with unconsciously in the company of others, even though these habits might be antisocial. It's important, when drawing this card, to look closely at your behavior and of those around you to check any habits that might be antisocial and which should be nipped in the bud – presupposing that at some point The Hermit may wish to re-enter a more conventional version of society.

The Hermit, as well as being an antisocial, nature-loving loner, is also often seen as a guru, her self-imposed solitude a spiritual quest of some sort. And it's true that time spent alone can result in great insights – but it's important to find balance, and above all The Hermit needs to bear this in mind and know that his or her fellow human beings are an equal and necessary part of the equation.

10
THE WHEEL OF FORTUNE

La Ruota

The Swallow

"As the blazing fire reduces wood to ashes, similarly, the fire of self-knowledge reduces all karma to ashes."
~Bhagavad Gita

KEYWORDS
Destiny, luck, joy, synchronicity, completion, inevitability, a harvest, a conclusion

DESCRIPTION
In the forefront of the picture stands a beautiful woman. She wears a pink top, a red belt and a blue skirt. She has black hair and

violet eyes, and her hands are clasped casually behind her head. Maybe she's doing something to her hair? Behind her head, halo-like, is a golden disc. There's a face visible within this disc. Curiously, behind the woman is a huge pair of white wings. From the bottom of the wings, at the right-hand side of the card, emerges a hand which holds another golden disc. This disc is split into eight segments. The hand also holds a pink-white flower, a lily. Another lily appears in the right-hand corner of the card.

Along the uppermost part of the picture, which is an unfathomable black, hang some pieces of fruit. There are three of the swallows that personify the idea of The Wheel of Fortune. They fly upwards across the picture, from left to right.

THE WHEEL OF FORTUNE AND THE SWALLOW

The swallow appears all over the world, and is universally regarded as a harbinger of spring; a sign that the wheel of the year, like the wheel of fortune, turns full circle. The sighting of the first swallow is a very welcome one, a sign that better weather is approaching, but of course we've got to remember the old saying that "one swallow doesn't make a summer," and it's true that we never know precisely what the wheel of fortune holds for us. Despite our fascination with looking into the "future" or trying to divine what's ahead, it's essential that there are surprises in our lives. These days, the appearance of the swallows is changing in some parts of the world due to global warming; even our planet is subject to unexpected change.

The discovery of fire – and carbon-generated energy of all kinds – has of course had a profound effect on the planet. The swallow, in many folk tales from around the world, is believed to be one of the birds that were responsible for bringing fire to mankind. Native American belief lyrically explains how the swallow stole a little bit of the Sun in order to bless mankind with the gift of fire. This further underscores its affinity with The Wheel of Fortune card.

Before we knew about the migratory patterns

of birds, there were some weird antique theories about what happened to them in the winter. Possibly the most far-fetched was that they lived on the moon! New scientific discoveries everyday tell us the truth about how our planet works, but folk belief and superstition still carry a lot of weight, and despite our educated circumstances there are many irrational beliefs that hold great sway over us.

The Significance of The Wheel of Fortune and the Swallow

The Wheel of Fortune is a reminder that our circumstances may change, and that we need to retain our personal integrity and the values that shape us as individuals, whatever those changes might be. It's also an apposite reminder that whilst change can be shocking, unexpected, exciting, or horrific, it is above all a good thing. Who wants to be stuck in a rut, after all?

A belief in past lives and reincarnation is common throughout the world, and indeed, was even common currency in the Western World prior to the general conversion to Christianity. However, the idea of "something next" is a red herring, because none of us can ever know anything for certain. The Swallow, as a bird that circles The Wheel of Fortune, reminds us that we have to live for the day, to see the best in all circumstances, and to exert mind over matter. The only thing we can really change is our mind and our attitude.

The Wheel of Fortune also tells another tale, of cause and effect. Earlier, we looked at the consequences of global warming, an instance of this if ever there was one. This card is also a reminder of the karmic balance in human lives, too. Good turns and favors done for people, selflessly and without a thought of them being repaid, are generally the acts of people whose lives are balanced enough for them to recognize that a good turn done for one is a good turn done for all. Inevitably, this currency will be repaid during testing times. This card also speaks of unconditional love, born not of wanting or needing, but simply enjoying someone for who they are, without wanting them to change.

The change wrought by the Wheel of Fortune can also represent a harvest, the currency brought about by all those good turns or even bad turns. There's the need for summing-up, an audit of the past, and the resolution needed, before we can go forward, unencumbered, into the future. The swallow speaks to us of the tender feelings towards an old love, and the trepidation and excitement of the new, and the bit in between where we might be alone, an opportunity to stand on our own two feet and rediscover who we are, something that can get lost within a close partnership.

This is a very good card, since it indicates a period of intense learning and the opportunity to emerge, butterfly-like, from the chrysalis of the past.

THE WHEEL OF FORTUNE REVERSED

A wheel doesn't exactly have a reverse position, but here's an analysis nevertheless. Sometimes, the events precipitated by The Wheel of Fortune might not seem "fair." You might want to bemoan your fate and decide that this is because of events from a past life, or you might relish everything as an opportunity simply because it's a privilege to be alive, healthy, vertical, and standing firm upon this incredible planet. The Wheel of Fortune asks you to really examine yourself and decide which it's to be. You can spiral inward, towards despair, or you can turn that spiral outwards and embrace what's in store for you. No matter how we interpret The Wheel of Fortune, ultimately, it's up to us to decide how we should approach it. Have courage!

11
JUSTICE

La Guistizia
The Ostrich

"Injustice anywhere is a threat to justice everywhere."
         ~Martin Luther King, Jr.

KEYWORDS
Balance, harmony, truth, equity, fairness, impartiality, poise, discrimination, clarity, correct action

DESCRIPTION
A beautiful older woman, with a welcoming expression on her face, stands in the forefront of this picture. She wears a blue dress. The sword and scales – archetypal symbols of justice – appear in front of her. Behind her, to her

right, appears the head of a tiger which has its paw placed protectively over her left shoulder. This paw appears to be grasping the scales. The woman wears two distinct symbols on the right side of her dress; the astrological symbols for both Libra and Sagittarius.

The bird that represents the concept of justice is the ostrich, and two of these huge birds loom behind the woman. They have the proud, haughty demeanor that's typical of the bird.

In the golden background of the picture, at the top left-hand side, are ten stars. These ten stars are mirrored over the heads of the woman and the tiger.

Justice and the Ostrich

Ma'at, the Egyptian Goddess of law and justice, is always depicted wearing an ostrich feather. And when the hearts of the deceased were brought before Osiris to be judged in the Afterworld, these same hearts were measured against an ostrich feather. The reason for this is that in contrast to feathers from other birds, which cannot be symmetrical since they are engineered for flight, both sides of the feather of the flightless ostrich are perfectly balanced. It's likely that the beauty of the feather rather than just its symmetry made it a favorite of the Pharaohs.

In terms of the symbolism of any bird, its defining quality is that it flies. Imagine that you're a bird for a moment. Flightlessness, like justice, is hugely frustrating.

There are a few unjust and prejudiced opinions about the ostrich, too. For example, we say that someone buries their head in the sand, like an ostrich, if there's something to avoid. But this is wrong; the ostrich exhibits no such behavior. The ostriches share one large hole in the ground in which to bury all their eggs, collectively. If the cache of eggs is threatened in any way then the bird will flatten its head against the ground to hide the eggs. Also, it's not fair or just to say that the ostrich is stupid because of its habit of eating small stones. The bird swallows grit to help its digestion. However, like the magpie, the ostrich is attracted to shiny objects; bits of metal, glass, etc. The bird gobbles these down without any adverse effects and this is the reason that the bird is sometimes depicted with a key in its beak.

Both these fallacies are a reminder that justice can be a difficult thing to define, and we need to ask questions and be dispassionate in order to discover the truth.

Justice and the Ostrich

What exactly is justice? For all that it's meant to be the product of impartiality, true objectivity – and a real understanding of the facts – can be very tricky. In a court of law, there are certain aspects that cannot be taken into account which nevertheless could have an important part to play when we're trying to color in a picture, when we're trying to gain a three-dimensional view of a case. This is exactly why the law operates under such a rigid code, designed to exclude any inkling of human subjectivity.

The scales are ancient as a symbol of justice, and we've seen how they were used as such as far back as the Egyptians. Where this card appears, it can indicate a necessity for a decision to be made; a decision that needs to be made with the head, not the heart; a decision that needs to be thought out with a mind that's as keen as the sharp blade of the sword that also symbolizes the idea of justice.

A key word for this card is "discrimination." This implies taking a long-term view of events and finding the peaceful place inside you that tells you whether or not you are making the right decision. You know that you have the clarity that will enable you to discern the right course of action, and that this clarity will be matched by the inner calmness that speaks of an easy conscience. It might also be the case that part of your decision needs to take into account the vagaries and madness of other people, and you might decide that such vagaries are not your problem; this might seem harsh or contrary to your usual way of doing things, and could be something in yourself that requires deep, logical analysis. And this isn't always easy on your own. You might be thinking of consulting with an outside agent who can help you toward true justice – maybe a legal professional, or maybe a councilor of some description.

There's a question that might be cropping up for you right now; "why?" Sometimes events are hard to fathom or make sense of. It's no coincidence that this card follows The Wheel of Fortune, which can force us to ask that same question. And the same rules apply here that applied with The Wheel of Fortune. It comes down to your attitude. There are some things that can never be explained because there is no discernable reason for them. The lesson here is that sometimes, we simply have to accept some things and forget about trying to explain them.

The other thing that needs to be taken into account is that, whilst there is a simple enough moral code that applies to all human beings, different religious beliefs have sets of rules all their own, the reasons for which can seem stupid or unfathomable to outsiders. We need to take these factors into account.

JUSTICE REVERSED

The law is designed to operate outside of the auspices of human fallibility and subjectivity. However, we *are* human, and human beings invented the concept of justice. And in order for real justice to be done, we need to understand the rules very well so that we can break them once in a while where necessary. After all, these rules are meant to work for justice, not against it. One person cannot be both judge and jury, but maybe that's what's happening at the moment. It may be that you are sometimes too rigid, and that it's time for some flexibility. It's as well, also, to bear in mind that not everyone follows the rules and patterns of "normal" behavior. If this rings any bells, then it might be time for you to apply some compassionate understanding to a particular situation.

12
THE HANGING MAN

L'Appeso

Pelican

"Rock bottom can be a great place to be, because it gives you a solid base to work from."

~Mark Townsend

KEYWORDS
Suspense, change, sacrifice, waiting, regeneration, rebirth, wisdom, prophecy

DESCRIPTION
A man, suspended from his left foot, dangles in the left-hand side of the painting. He's dressed quite foppishly in a lilac/purple suit and pale blue shoes. The gibbet, also violet, separates the man from the right-

hand side of the picture, which he is looking towards.

In the top right-hand corner of the painting we see the black lunar disc, surrounded by a bright umbra. This is the dark side of the moon. A space rocket flies up towards it.

The bird that represents the idea of The Hanging Man is the pelican, and a single bird stands between the two separate sides of the picture.

THE HANGING MAN AND THE PELICAN

In alchemical symbolism, the pelican has a great deal of significance. The bird represents the idea of the destruction of the old that's necessary to make way for the new, and this is also an important aspect of The Hanging Man; the need for a difficult process to trigger an initiation of some kind. The pelican, because of its supposed habit of piercing its own breast to feed its young, signifies self-sacrifice and deliberate loss of the ego, and this symbolism belongs not only to alchemical works but to the Christian faith, as a parallel to the sacrifice made by Christ. Now, the reddish staining on the breast of the pelican that was believed to be some sort of sacrificial blood is in fact caused by spittle. But this is a good example of how a natural and easily-explicable phenomenon is turned into a very different idea with the application of a vivid human imagination. Arguably, this is the same imagination that made a higher power in the first place. It is the same sort of imagination that was triggered when The Hanging Man, helplessly suspended, is forced to turn to his own internal resources which can then become the source of a momentous discovery.

The pelican itself is one of the most ancient birds on the planet, and remains aged at over forty million years showing that the bird has changed very little since then. The Seri people of Northern California acknowledge the great age of the pelican in one of their creation myths, believing that the bird, called The Ancient of Pelican, was the creature that raised the land above the waters after the great deluge. So the bird has a historical connection, a timelessness born of such epic continuity. This is an appropriate reminder of the wisdom that is born of experience and age, and a capacity to embrace all circumstances and to wrench the positive from them; a significant lesson for The Hanging Man.

The Significance of The Hanging Man and the Pelican

As we've discussed, the pelican has a significant role to play in alchemy, which is the mysterious, ancient and arcane art of transmutation. This transmutation was traditionally meant to be the fairly straightforward turning of base metal (lead) into gold, but the alchemical world is full of secrets, metaphysical notions hiding behind something more worldly. The alchemical process undertaken by The Hanging Man is that of finding the "gold" within. This may mean different things to different people, but the ultimate search is for the true meaning of life, the reconciliation of mind, body, and spirit, and the true understanding of the connections between everything in the Universe. This might sound terribly grandiose, but often the simplest of things, the things that are right under our noses, can be the key to the greatest truths.

The process that The Hanging Man is enduring is a form of torture known as "baffling." The position he's in means that the entire world is turned upside down and there's absolutely nothing that he can do about it without outside help. This is akin to imprisonment; The Hanging Man has no idea how long this state of enforced suspension will last. In mythology, the Norse God, Odin, hung upside down from a tree for nine days and nights and it was during this time that he saw, reflected in a puddle, the shapes and symbols of the runes. It's fitting that the discovery of letters is accorded such mythic status, because they mark a profound switch in the consciousness of mankind. Letters are not simple shapes that represent sounds, but each individual squiggle symbolizes an entire concept within itself.

So, The Hanging Man card tells of a profound process of initiation, an accelerated learning that is brought about by seemingly adverse circumstances. It's essential to strip away the ego, to go back to rock bottom, and to trust in the process, no matter how difficult it might seem to be at the time. Odin's "bafflement" resulted in a great leap of reasoning, a stroke of inspiration which had far-reaching effects. The story of Odin can be found in real life, too; think of people whose imprisonment has resulted in great discoveries; Rudolf Steiner is a good example. The trick in making the most of baffling circumstances of your own is to acknowledge the situation you're in and surrender to it whole-heartedly, and be excited about the opportunities that it affords. Drawing such a card – and being in such a situation – is a privilege afforded those who are strong enough for it.

THE HANGING MAN REVERSED

Sometimes, when faced with adverse circumstances, we don't make the connection between cause and effect in our own lives. We blame other people or believe that situations beyond our control are the cause of the pickle we're in. It's time to take a good, long, hard look at everything in our lives, and to make a huge effort to be conscious that we are actually responsible for everything in it. This is not easy, since it requires a willing sublimation of the ego and, sometimes, to allow the world to turn upside down. But so long as you trust that everything happens in the right way and at the right time, and that change is truly possible, then the world will be yours.

13
DEATH

La Morte
The Vulture

"Live as if you were to die tomorrow. Learn as if you were to live forever."
~Mahatma Ghandi

KEYWORDS
Transformation, rebirth, change, en ending, a new era, new expectations, rewarded efforts

DESCRIPTION
A woman, dressed in red, floats, partially submerged, in a red and golden sea. She has a peaceful, slightly vacant look on her face, and although we might expect her eyes to be closed, as though dead, her eyes are open. She's conscious, aware, and knows where she's headed for.

She wears a black dress, with pink and red patterns. In her left hand she holds a pomegranate which is clearly raised above the churning sea.

The bird that personifies the idea of death is the vulture. There's a vulture-like bird on the woman's dress, and another vulture appears in the foreground of the picture, flying shadow-like beneath her.

Death and the Vulture

It's interesting that we associate the vulture with death; to us, when we see it circling the skies, it acts as a warning that death is near. However, the ancients had a different idea about the vulture. Perhaps this is because they had a more balanced and realistic notion about what death actually is, an inevitable and natural part of life, not an ending, but a simple transition. It's no accident that the Egyptians accorded the vultures' sacred status as The Pharaoh's Pets. This is because they were invaluable in keeping the streets clean and clear. Vultures were also honored as a deity in the form of the Goddess, Nekhbet, who guarded and protected all the Queens of Egypt. The Goddess Isis, too, is closely aligned with the bird, embraced by its wings and ready to suckle. This is because the vulture is renowned for its maternal instinct; therefore death is a return to the Great Mother, personified sometimes as the vulture.

There isn't really any such thing as death, only change and transformation. The body decays and its base chemical constituents are recycled, turned into something else from which new life can spring. The vulture, as a scavenging bird that never kills, is the ultimate recycler. For the Greeks and Romans, the vulture was one of the key messengers from the Gods, sacred to Apollo, and therefore an incredibly important omen. The appearance of twelve of the birds determined that Romulus was acknowledged as the founder of Rome rather than his twin brother, Remus. In Tibet, the vultures that consume the fleshy remains of the increasingly-rare sky burial are believed to take the souls of the dead straight back to the source. The birds only come to take away the remains when they are called, and not a scrap is left. The stripping of the flesh from the bones, for Buddhists, is analogous to the revelation of truth.

SIGNIFICANCE OF DEATH AND THE VULTURE

To the casual observer, the death card is probably the most feared of all the Tarot cards, and the most unwelcome one to appear in any spread. However, for experts and "proper" readers, there's absolutely no need for this to be the case. The card is a positive one and should be welcomed as such.

In the West, in particular, there's a tendency to "hide" from the idea of death, not to talk about it properly, as though we were ashamed of it and also the natural process of ageing. Both are inevitable, and to be welcomed. If we acknowledge both, properly, then we can liberate ourselves to get on with our lives, to live every day as though it were a work of art, taking joy in small things, and living in the moment.

The death card is not about an end as such, but rather about an intense change, a transformation. It can also represent an initiation, the sloughing off of the old in favor of the new, and the process that's needed to embrace such a change fully and completely. All the changes indicated by this card are positive, but require an effort of awareness and consciousness, a surrender of the ego. Hence, the girl in the card approaches the underworld with open eyes and is willing accept wherever the river is taking her. The process of initiation, in any culture, involves a "death" followed by a rebirth. Puberty, signifying the acceptance into adulthood, is a good example. The Death card signifies a time of elevated consciousness, a new ability to climb outside of the self and see the bigger picture. The high, effortless flight of vultures caused the Greeks to believe that they were born of the wind, and if we can put ourselves into this same state of willingness to surrender old ways and patterns then we can be reborn as fully integrated human beings; this is the magical process that Jung referred to as "individuation."

This card is also the card of sexual desire and procreation. The French call the orgasm "the little death," and real surrender to passion means that we have to cast aside our inhibitions and become free of the ego. This is why sexual liaisons in later life can often be much more beautiful and meaningful. As we approach the twin inevitabilities of the ageing process and of death, we can allow ourselves to be truly free. The process of sex also means that we have to subsume the self in the quest to become the sum of a greater part – two people as one, the ultimate alchemical process and a physical union that connects us, truly, as spirits. This card is a reminder that there's nothing to lose.

DEATH REVERSED

Sometimes, we resist the need for change. We might not even realize this is happening, but the manifestations include depression, allergies, alcoholism, putting on excess weight. It can be hard to see the wood for the trees; after all the deeper the rut the harder to see the horizon. Unless we can make the effort and have the courage to recognize what's happening, then life will certainly force changes upon us. The old way of life may be left behind forever and the process of changing might be difficult and painful, but, as the saying goes, we're a long time dead. Better to acknowledge any aspects of your life that are less than satisfactory, and make positive efforts toward making healthy changes.

14
TEMPERANCE

La Temperanza

The Robin

"Temperance; eat and carouse with Bacchus, or munch on dry bread with Jesus, but don't sit down without one of the Gods."
~D. H. Lawrence

KEYWORDS
Patience, harmony, frugality, compatibility, friendliness, good influences, calmness, sobriety, forces of good

DESCRIPTION
A girl, in a lilac dress decorated with small red flowers, sits on a branch high up in a tree. She hugs her knees and looks down modestly. The girl has wings, and her position in the tree

might imply that she is somewhere between human and divine. In the top right-hand corner of the picture is a small angelic figure, looking upwards. This figure mixes together liquids from two jugs, one red, one blue.

The bird that represents the notion of Temperance is the robin. Two robins appear in this picture. One is very obvious, perched in the foreground of the painting. The other isn't so obvious, and sits on the girl's toe. You can see that the robin's beak is open as though it's singing.

TEMPERANCE AND THE ROBIN

The robin is a welcome sight to everyone, having a very special place in our hearts, particularly in the middle of the winter when lots of other birds have flown to warmer climates. Robins come closer to us than many other wild birds, a risk that pays dividends as the gardener whose spade the robin perches on reveals an easy source of worms. Our relationship with the robin is an easy and effortless one, although this is one of the most territorial of birds and has no qualms about seeing off competition from others of his kind. The national emblem of the British Isles, it's no surprise that there are more stories about the robin than almost any other bird. It was a robin, for example, in the story "Babes in the Wood" that covered the children with leaves to keep them warm as they slept. There's a natural balance and symbiosis between us and the robin that makes it the bird that best represents the concept of Temperance.

The red breast of the robin means that it has a natural association with fire, and in legend, it's one of the birds that's credited with bringing fire to mankind. The angelic figure that appears in this card carries two jugs, one containing red liquid and the other blue. This represents the mixing of water and fire, spirit and matter; a fundamental alchemical process. In the Christian Church, the robin is associated with death and resurrection, probably because of its appearance in the winter months. It might be for this reason that many people believe that the appearance of the robin heralds the presence of a departed spirit. The appearance of a robin inside the house was once believed to presage a death in the family.

The Significance of Temperance and the Robin

One of the key messages of this Tarot card, which is about the close relationship between mankind and birds, is the need for ecological awareness and proper care of the planet. The need for Temperance in this instance is paramount. The way we live on this planet and the ways in which we react with the natural world have changed dramatically in a very short space of time; this isn't the place for an in-depth discussion of these issues; but just imagine how very different this planet would be without the motor car.

Temperance is about the need to find an operable balance whilst negotiating difficult factors – and it's also about the truth that it is simply not possible to keep everyone happy all of the time. We have to make sacrifices, or ask others to make sacrifices, for the greater good. To find a truly temperate solution to any problem means that it it's fairly inevitable that we might risk upsetting and disappointing others, but with the application of Temperance, discretion, and a truthfully convincing argument, we can limit any upset and hope that the other person is reasonable enough to see sense. This need to achieve balance is an ongoing process that needs concentration and an ability to be "in the moment" in order to be fully aware of what's really necessary.

The Temperance/robin card melds together the lessons learned by all the other cards in the Tarot; the need to be The Fool as well as the father, for example; the Temperance card reminds us that all the facets of the characters we meet in a Tarot deck are all different aspects of ourselves. We can pull into focus the part that is needed without forgetting who we are and what we want. This card is the "toolbox" of the Tarot, the card that inspires us to illumination and realization, as startling and welcoming a sight as that robin in the snow. In drawing this card we become aware of all the colors that combine in our one self. It also speaks of the integration of matter and spirit, intuition and the intellect, the lighter side of our soul with the shadow part, each of which highlights the other equally.

TEMPERANCE REVERSED

It's possible that you are in a situation where you are sublimating your needs in order to encompass the needs of others. This is never a long-term solution and will result in dissatisfaction and resentment. You need to question why you find it so easy to relinquish control of your own life and you need to wrest back that control. Lack of self-confidence is caused by a crisis of ego that is just as unreasonable in someone who has the opposite quality, of arrogance. There needs to be a midway point or common ground between the two. Again, this requires effort, vigilance and honesty. If there's any chance that you are uncertain of what you really want, then spend some time alone and examine your heart.

15
THE DEVIL

Il Diavolo
The Magpie

"He who does not see the angels and devils in the beauty and malice of life will be far removed from knowledge, and his spirit will be empty of affection."
~Kahlil Gibran

KEYWORDS
Materialism, mortality, sexuality, dualism, dependence, realization of responsibility, mischievousness

DESCRIPTION
The colors on this card are predominantly red. Right at the front of the painting appears the bird that personifies the nature of The Devil;

that is, the magpie, a member of the ultra-intelligent corvid family, which also includes the raven, the crow, and the jay. The magpie is grasping one of five golden coins in its bill.

Behind the magpie, looking over her shoulder with a furtive expression, is a young woman. Dressed in red, she clutches a red serpent.

Around her neck is a necklace – or is it? Look again and you'll see it's a chain. The other end of the chain is held by a male figure, who stands firmly inside a pale blue disc with a red umbra. The background color for this card is golden-red.

THE DEVIL AND THE MAGPIE

Perhaps the magpie's most distinctive character trait is the bird's predilection to steal bright, shiny objects. But it's unlikely that the magpie sees that it is a thief. The concept is alien to magpies, and this throws up an interesting argument about morals and morality. We believe that The Devil is evil, but does The Devil believe this too? In Britain, popular superstition associates the magpie with The Devil and consequently, charms and obeisances are paid to the bird to dispel any evil that it may carry in its wake. In Scotland, the bird was even supposed to have a drop of the "de'il's blood" on its tongue, and the prejudice against the bird was probably due to the influence of the early Christian Church. Indeed, there's a myth that the magpie refused to get into the Arc with all the other birds and animals, preferring instead to berate the passengers from the roof, chattering and squawking.

As befits the personification of devilry and the material world, the magpie sports a very handsome and elegant livery. The sharply-contrasting "uniform" of the bird stands for dualism and the constant battle between forces of light and darkness. In Scandinavia, the legendary dark magic of the magpie continues; it's believed that the birds turn into sorcerers on Walpurgisnacht, and also that magpies either appear as witches or are used by them as transport.

The ancient Greeks and Romans associated the magpie with Dionysus/Bacchus, the God of drinking and revelry. An excess of alcohol, of course, loosens tongues, often a cause of trouble and conflict. The horned God of drinking and revelry is one of the early prototypes for the devils and demons of today, the original nature gods rendered evil by the early Christian church.

Significance of the Devil and the Magpie

This is another one of the cards that people generally don't like to see in a spread. But this prejudice needs to be addressed; we need to look beyond the accepted beliefs about what a devil is, or what we might have been told about its nature.

Essentially, this card is all about the attractions and delights of the material world. And there should be no problem with this. This is the world in which we live. We are made of matter, we react with matter. It might be true that we are all made of stardust, but stardust itself is matter. Material delights, sexual encounters, and the pleasures of the flesh are all an important part of our world, but it's important that they are balanced by an equal measure of spirit. The figure with the chains that appears in the disc holds those chains quite loosely; unlike the magpie, who has no concept of thievery and operates outside the moral and ethical code of human beings, we do have consciousness and the ability to make deliberate choices. These choices are nothing to do with religion, but about the basic rules that make for a healthy society. Animals mate according to the seasons and the necessity to reproduce. Human beings can choose whether or not to mate or to procreate, and both sexual desire and practice should not, as a rule, be divorced from finer feelings of love and affection. The permissive society and "free love" prevalent in the 1960s was indeed a liberation, but resulted in a generation of dysfunctionality and the break-down of simple family values.

The magpie's fondness for shiny things is another aspect that links it to The Devil. The accumulation of wealth for its own sake is to be regarded with suspicion, since money alone means nothing. It's what can be done with wealth that makes it valuable, an exchange of energy that's about balance rather than greed. A good example of the evil that can be caused by wealth is the arguments that families have over an inheritance, since the money is inevitably equated to affection. There's nothing wrong in essence with having the ability to make money, to reap the rewards of hard work, but an overemphasis on the cash as the endgame can result in a miserly attitude to life. It's also funny how the accumulation of cash and sexual attractiveness are often inextricably linked. We even convince ourselves that money can make us happy, but this isn't the case at all. It's a delusion. In drawing this card, it's possible that we need to take a step back and re-examine our priorities in life, to ask whether we are putting too much stress on material things. It might be time to let the simpler things in life come to the fore for a change. And remember, some of the glittering things collected by that magpie might be gold – but it's just as likely to be the odd bit of tinfoil. The magpie, unlike the man, is pleased with either.

THE MAGPIE REVERSED

The material world, and the emphasis on riches as a status symbol, can become a trap. The more we have, the more we have to maintain. Credit card debts are a good example of this. The desire for things, for more and more "stuff," can spiral out of control, and the reasons for having those things can become increasingly meaningless. We think we need them, but we don't. We don't need to be ruled by advertisements, or envy for what our friends and neighbors might possess. Similarly, rather than seeking the qualities we lack in other people, we should try to find them or develop them in ourselves. It's time for us to work on ourselves to become fully rounded human beings, self-sufficient and aware of the priorities in life. It might be time to enjoy the true liberation that comes with giving, whether that's material goods, your time, or your heart.

16
THE TOWER

La Torre

The Raven

"The lofty pine is oftenest shaken by the winds; High towers fall with a heavier crash; And the lightning strikes the highest mountain."

~Horace

KEYWORDS
A sudden or shocking event, change, deception, illumination, realization, awakening, intelligence, destruction and creation

DESCRIPTION
A woman in a pink dress lies in a collapsed position in the center of the picture, eyes closed as though she's unconscious. Through the

window behind her we see two towers. The one on the left is flaming dramatically, and the one on the right appears as a dark shadow. The sky above is blackened with smoke, although it's a clear blue at a lower level.

The bird that personifies the idea of The Tower is the raven, and a lone raven appears here, perching on the hip of the collapsed woman. Its beak is open and it's evidently squawking. In the very front of the picture is a cat, relaxing in the way that only cats can, echoing the pose of the woman. The cat has one eye open.

Pieces of fruit – primarily pears – also appear in the picture. One of the apples has been sliced, revealing the five-pointed star that has a multitude of meanings. Right by the woman's elbow is a pomegranate, also sliced open.

THE TOWER AND THE RAVEN

The raven. The "bird of cunning," the trickster. All over the world, the primary belief about the raven is in its magical powers, its qualities of sorcery, mischief, and transformation. Prodigiously intelligent, the average I.Q. of the bird is way higher than that of the average human being. Ravens can make tools, can solve problems. Pliny relates a story of how a raven, unable to reach far enough into a container to drink the water inside, dropped stones into the pot to raise the water level. Ravens play freely, and have their own sophisticated language which is not only verbal, but physical. Ravens are able to communicate their moods and desires with a unique form of body language.

Ravens have long been associated with the Tower of London. Indeed, their original appearance is entrenched in a mysterious Celtic legend. A Welsh King, Bran, (whose name means raven) was the protector of the whole of Britain. His sister, who was being mistreated by her husband, an Irish monarch, managed to send a message via a starling to Bran to explain her predicament. This resulted in a mighty battle and Bran's subsequent decapitation. Bran's head, however, was still able to speak, uttering prophecies, and the head demanded that it be buried at Tower Hill. The Tower of London was built on that hill, and the legend says that so long as ravens are present at the Tower there in honour of their kingly namesake, then Britain will always be protected from invasion by her enemies. The superstition about these ravens is so strong that during the Second World War when the raven population was depleted, Winston Churchill sent for urgent replacement birds, appropriately enough, from the mountains of Wales.

The blackness of the raven means that it's sometimes interpreted as a gloomy sign, but in the Native American belief, the sheer glitter and shine of the bird is what counts. There, it's seen as the creator of the Sun and bringer of light, an apposite reminder that it's not always necessary to be alarmed by the sight of The Tower card in a spread.

Significance of The Tower and the Raven

A tower is a citadel, a fortress, a safe place. A tower is built to be strong, used as a place to both defend and attack, and the necessity for a tower presupposes that there must be riches of some kind in the vicinity. The person or people who had the wherewithal to build The Tower must be comfortable, secure, and powerful. They must occupy a very secure and protected position in life.

We speak of people in "ivory towers" as being unapproachable, living in a rarefied atmosphere, untouched by the "lower" world, and complacent.

Therefore, the destruction of a tower is a momentous event, shocking, calamitous, everything turned upside down and destroyed. When the Twin Towers were destroyed, amidst the sheer horror about the lives that were lost was the underlying awe that such a strong symbol of America's power and wealth were destroyed in such an apocryphal way.

In this case, perceived wealth and riches may not be exactly what they appear to be. The greater the wealth, after all, the greater the responsibility and the worry. And sometimes we put too much emphasis on wealth, often to the detriment of the things that really matter. When this symbolic tower is swept away, the foundations that are exposed are a reminder of the real meaning of life and what's important. In the card, the girl sleeps as peacefully as her cat and hasn't a care in the world.

However, The Tower isn't just about material wealth. It also signifies the world of intellect and ideas. Destruction of The Tower in this sense signifies a shake-up of accepted ways of thinking and the need to embrace new ideas that might be radical or that might require us to adjust long-accepted constructs. This too requires a leap of faith; and maybe it *is* possible to teach old dogs new tricks!

This card tells a story of destruction and creation; another suitable bird for this card could have been the phoenix. The "blow" might be as dramatic as the collapse of wealth, or it might take the form of a sudden lightning-bolt of inspiration. When for example an apple landed on Newton's head, this seemingly insignificant event cast very wide ripples; this is the sort of effect presaged by The Tower – a real "Eureka!" moment. Old ideas were swept away in favor of the new. The "eureka" might take a little time to come following the aftermath of events, after the dust has settled. Whatever form it takes, this dramatically unexpected event will strip away the layers of the ego and the material self, allowing the spirit to emerge unscathed, bigger, better, and brighter than before. However, despite the deep shock, the events described by this card can cause, ultimately The Tower/Raven is the card of ultimate liberation, self-realization and deep joy.

THE TOWER REVERSED

It might be that you feel events are running completely and utterly beyond your control, and it's hard to keep up, both mentally and physically. It's possible that you are trying to cope with difficult situations all alone, and it's time to seek help. It is now the time to relinquish pride and think about what you need for your own health. After all, you can do nothing for anyone unless you yourself are healthy. Seek some help, step aside from whatever situation is causing so much anguish, and try to gain some perspective so that you can come back to it invigorated, refreshed, renewed.

17
THE STAR

LA STELLA
THE NIGHTINGALE

"People they come together, people they fall apart, no-one can stop us now, 'cause we are all made of stars."

~Moby

KEYWORDS

Hope, inspiration, bright future, opportunity, happiness, spiritual love, past and present united, astrological influence

DESCRIPTION

Against a dark night or early morning sky we see a nightingale, the bird that personifies the idea of The Star, perched on a branch, singing. Seven pomegranates hang amongst

the branches around the bird. A bright white star appears in the sky just below the bird.

A woman, with long blonde hair, is watching the nightingale in admiration. She's wearing a blue dress covered with yellow stars, and has a further five-pointed star painted on her right cheekbone.

In the foreground of the picture are two jugs. One has red designs of a five-pointed star, and the other is smaller, blue and yellow, decorated with a question mark.

THE STAR AND THE NIGHTINGALE

In the same way that the stars are still in the sky during the daytime when we can't see them, the nightingale does sing during the day, too, although it is when it sings when the sky is dark that we hear it most clearly – away from the sound of the other birds and in the still air of the night, at a time when no other birds make a sound. Unlike other birds, the nightingale sings all alone, and this might seem melancholy; however, like The Star card itself, the nightingale's lovely singing in the dark is more often taken as a symbol of hope. The Latin name for the nightingale is "Lucerna," from the same root as the word for "light." This is because the nightingale heralds the dawn with her song, and also underlines the connection, here, with the light from the stars.

There's an Italian legend that explains precisely why the nightingale has such a lovely voice. When God was giving all the other birds their brilliant colors, the nightingale was last in the queue and there were no colors left for her. So God compensated for this by bestowing upon her the gift of song. The Arabs believed that the nightingale would continue to sing until it died.

Despite its unassuming appearance, the plain little nightingale has such a reputation for fine music that Paganini said that Stradivarius made his celebrated violins "from the trees on which the nightingales sing." This is of course an analogy.

The Significance of The Star and The Nightingale

In many depictions of this card there's a huge, glittering fixed star surrounded by seven planets. Here those seven planets are represented by the pomegranates, symbols of the Underworld, which are nevertheless still illuminated by the little stars that are shining on the surfaces of their skins.

If The Tower was a bolt from the blue in terms of inspiration, the star could be said to be a more tranquil journey towards realization, when we have enough perspective to be able to see precisely why certain things happened when they did. The Star gives us the benefit, for example, of seeing the truth and the reason as to why those towers were destroyed. This is the lucidity that the nightingale's name, Lucerna, refers to, and it's possible that drawing this card means that you will soon experience a series of lucid dreams that will enable you to integrate and process many of the things that have happened to you. It might also be a time to seek professional help with an analysis of the events that have brought you to your current position, which is more settled, tranquil and harmonious than it perhaps has been. It would be appropriate to seek the help of a professional astrologer. As well as a source of inspiration, the Star is the source of illumination.

The Star is also all about the gentle and healing powers of the element of water. Emotional trauma can be soothed by bathing or swimming, the water connecting us with the mother Goddess, the Great Mother. The flow of the waters here is a reminder of the "flow" of our lives, which, like the stars, is always there whether or not we can "feel" it. In drawing this card it's likely that you are lucky enough to be feeling this "flow" and that you are experiencing the serendipitous events and meaningful coincidences that are a unique reminder that you're doing the right thing at the right time. The Star connects us with the life-force, reminds us of the interconnectedness of all things. The stars in the sky are believed to not only reflect but to influence our lives, and it might be that in drawing this card there might be an interest in matters astrological.

THE STAR REVERSED

Although we have to believe that we are always on the right path, sometimes we ignore our instincts and we can go astray. The "flow" of the Universe always includes us in its waters, but it requires constant vigilance to make sure that we are aware enough to make the right choices. Lies, deceits, and delusion will throw us off that course, morally speaking. There are influences around you that may be worth investigating more thoroughly and it could be that there are influences around you which are not as beneficial as you think. Knowing that you are made of stars, learn to use your inner light of intuition to get you back to where you need to be. Experiment with your dreams and ask for guidance.

18
THE MOON

La Luna
The Swan

"The Swan, like the soul of the poet, by the dull world is ill understood..."
~Henirich Heine
from "Evening Song"

KEYWORDS
The subconscious mind, psychic awakening, the Dreamworld, feminine intuition, the emotions

DESCRIPTION
A beautiful woman with wild red hair looks back at us from behind the wing of a swan. Beads in her hair spell "LEDA," a reminder of the Greek myth in which the God, Zeus, took

on the form of the bird in order to seduce the beautiful daughter of the Spartan King, Tyndareus. The resulting offspring included Helen of Troy. The golden collar around the neck of the Swan bears the name of Leda's supernatural lover. The crayfish on the wing of the swan is a nod to one of the traditional symbols of the Moon card, and the Moon itself appears in the top right hand corner of the picture, in crescent form.

THE MOON AND THE SWAN

Since both are epitome of the feminine aspect and the element of water, the moon, and the swan are inextricably linked. Physically, the silky, milky glow of the swan on the water even looks like the full moon, the curve of its wings reminiscent of the crescent phase. A recurrent theme in swan mythology right across the planet is its shapeshifting abilities – again, an attribute of the changeable quality of the waxing, full and waning lunar disc which itself symbolizes the Triple Goddess.

One of the best-known of these swan/human/shapeshifting tales is the story of Leda, who, despite being married, is lusted after by the virile God, Zeus. Zeus transforms himself into a swan and seduces her, and Leda bears twins, Castor and Pollux.

In alchemy, the swan is the symbol for the second phase of the process of transmutation, also known as The Whitening. This is the metaphorical brightening of the inner world after the painful separation effected by the first phase, or Blackening, and results in the unification of the physical and spiritual worlds. Again, in myth, the swan is the bird that bridges the gap between our world and the unseen world, hence its ability to transform into a human being in so many stories. Water, too, symbolizes the world of spirit; reflective, moving, mysterious. One particular role of the swan was to carry the souls of unborn children into this parallel Otherworld to which water provided an access portal.

In Ancient Greece, the swan was dedicated to the Muses, the immortals who inspired music, poetry, and song, and appropriately, the swan is the bird most closely linked to all matters poetic. When Apollo, the God of poetry and prophecy, was born, seven swans flew seven times around his island. And the poetic Irish Goddess, Brigid, is symbolized by the white swan, her territory described as the "swan-abounding land." In honor of their Muse, the druidic bards wore cloaks of swans' feathers, which conferred shamanistic powers to the wearer.

Significance of The Moon and the Swan

In many interpretations of The Tarot, The Moon carries a dark and often bleak message. This is because The Moon, as the feminine aspect, is a reflection of the masculinity of The Sun; if The Sun is the bright side of the psyche, then The Moon is the dark. The good news is that the "dark night of the soul," which is an aspect of the card, might be the most difficult part of initiation, but in drawing this card, it means that we are ready to face whatever might be put in front of us. Before us is an unknown, daunting world, but we know that what came before is now almost fully integrated and that we have one last "twist" that will reconcile everything we are and the sum total of our experiences. The greater the fear, the more profound the learning experience that we are about to approach. The Moon, in all its nocturnal mystery, marks entry into an unknown world, the psychological past also a foreign country. Here, we are in the no-mans' land between what went before and what lies ahead, in a dreamscape of strange creatures and alarming sounds.

However, soon the weirdness of the new environment starts to become more comfortable. As the swan is the shapeshifter, the bird is a reminder that we can shapeshift too; we can transform ourselves in full consciousness whilst retaining the essence of what we really are. The Moon tells us that we are going through a process of becoming bigger, better, and brighter than before, although in order to do so we might go through a period of isolation and disorientation as all the old ways fall back. Now it's time to learn to stand on our own two feet, not to rely on anyone else for emotional support, but to discover that we have inner resources that are more powerful than we could ever have imagined. You might have tried to resist the changes presaged by this card, but now you can accept that this resistance itself was a necessary part of your journey. Once this is properly understood, you can allow yourself to feel a sense of relief; the new horizons that await beyond the dark can be anticipated not only with trepidation, but with excitement.

THE MOON REVERSED

We can build all sorts of walls around ourselves as a way of avoiding change. The more lies we tell to others and ourselves the more dangerously deluded we become as we start to believe these untruths, desperate to clinging to the old ways. There are many ways of avoiding the truth: drug addiction, alcoholism, consumerism. It's time to strip away all these conceits and realize that the essence of what you are deserves better than this. Be your own best counselor and trust that everything that has happened, every obstacle that you have placed in the path of your own development, has been for a reason. This is the time for your life to transform for the better – but it will require you to transcend your ego and let go of your fears.

19
THE SUN

Il Sole
The Peacock

"You cannot, in human experience, rush into the light. You have to go through the twilight into the broadening day before the noon comes and the full sun is upon the landscape."
~Woodrow Wilson

KEYWORDS
Creativity, beauty, inspiration, energy, success, clarity, contentment, success, love, sincerity, satisfaction

DESCRIPTION
A flame-haired woman appears in this painting, one hand raised to her forehead. The background is lavish gold. The flaming orb of

the sun that appears in the top right-hand corner of the picture matches the fiery mane of the woman. She wears golden jewelry, earrings and a pendant, which also show solar images. Her eyes are green.

In the foreground of the picture we see the peacock that personifies the many aspects of The Sun card. The bird sits, plump and resplendent, its train of iridescent feathers plainly showing those distinctive "eyes" though its furled.

At the bottom of the picture is the outstretched hand of a child.

THE SUN AND THE PEACOCK

The Peacock is the bird of the Goddess, Hera, Queen of the Sky. And it's true that, more than any other real bird, the stunning colors and splendor of the peacock shine just like The Sun, the card that belongs to this bird. The mythos of the peacock is colossal, as you might imagine. The Peacock Angel, in an obscure sect followed by some Kurdish peoples, equates to the brightest of all the angels, Lucifer. They don't see Lucifer as the personification of evil, but rather as the chief Archangel and the creator of the material world, foremost amongst the messengers of God and cast out of heaven at the same time as Adam and Eve.

The glory of the peacock makes it a favorite with royalty, and as well as belonging to the Sky Queen, the bird belongs to Kings, too. One of the most famous examples is the Shah Jahan, whose peacock throne was preposterously splendid, made of gold-covered marble and encrusted with every kind of precious gem you could possibly imagine.

The fire of the Sun is cathartic, and the Latin name for the bird, Pavo, means "purity" since the bird was legendarily believed to be able to neutralize poisons. The Sun card is about renewal and purity, traditionally symbolized by a little child; in this card the child's hand is a nod to the older imagery.

In alchemy, the process of transmutation of the soul, which is analogous to turning base metal into gold, the peacock sits in the center of the five birds that signify the different stages in the process. In a nutshell, this is all about awakening to the inner world, realizing that we exist beyond the limits of what we call time, and that the material world is an illusion. We need to look at things in a different way. Whilst acknowledging the immense achievement of scientific knowledge, it's still valid to know that, to some of our ancestors, The Sun was perceived as a hole in the sky through which the brilliant light of creation – the "Big Bang" – poured through, its bounty and benevolence enabling life on earth to exist.

SIGNIFICANCE OF THE SUN AND THE PEACOCK

If the moon/swan card represents the dark night of the soul, the final time in the wilderness and the long walk towards the light at the end of the tunnel, then The Sun appears just at that final moment of The Moon's reign; The Sun appears as a silver lining of hope and then bursts brilliantly into light, allowing us all to bask in its brilliant radiance.

The Sun/Peacock card is genuinely propitious. It is triumph over tragedy, a happy ending, joy, enlightenment gained after hardship, and even because of it. Although we know that the wheel always turns, once we've experienced the warm loving embrace of sunshine, we'll never forget it, and this experience will give us courage and perspective during any future cloudy times.

The Sun brings us back to a childlike state of mind, when every day of the Summer was full of sunlight and we enjoyed a carefree innocence. This is before the first trauma and the development of the full-blown adult ego. This "inner child" is always a part of us, always there, although covered in layers, laden with experience, memories, sadness, disappointment. In many ways this card bears similarities to The Fool, except with the benefit of applied experience rather than sheer happenstance. Here, our passions, interests, and talents are honed by the discipline of the skills we have learned. Imagine the dedication required to become a virtuoso pianist, for example; years of difficult toil until the music becomes effortless, joyful, liberating to both the player and the audience.

The Sun/Peacock is the contribution we can give to the world to make it a better place. It's about defining our personal philosophy and codes of living from the experiences we have of the world. If new horizons are beckoning, then follow your instincts and go for it. This card tells you that there's nothing to lose, that all experience is valuable, and it's never too late for anything. You're never too old to follow a passion or learn a new skill – or even to fall in love.

THE SUN REVERSED

Sometimes, no matter how intelligent, talented or able we are, something holds us back from making our dreams manifest in the real world. We might hold back believing the time isn't right, or we might blame the needs of a partner or children, or might otherwise make other people the excuse for our failure to fulfill potential. It's time now to realize that there are no barriers except for the ones that we have imposed on ourselves, and that there are no excuses anymore. We have to ask, is it fear of failure that stops us from trying – or is it fear of success? And what is there to lose? The only real risk is in taking no risk at all. Get on with it! Shine! Life is sweet – but life is short.

20
JUDGEMENT

Il Giudizio

The Crane

"...Judge a tree from its fruit, not its leaves..."

~Euripides

KEYWORDS

Accountability, longevity, rebirth, responsibility, a difficult situation, fatalism, an outcome awaited, guidance

DESCRIPTION

A young woman, blonde hair awry, lies sleeping against a background of gold and black. In her right hand she holds a glass of red wine, which she has spilled. Her naked form is partially veiled with a gauzy cloth that's patterned with red roses.

Against the blue sky in the top right hand corner of the picture we can see the leaves of a rowan tree. Pieces of fruit – apples, pears, and an orange – hang from the tree.

A small angel, haloed and with wings, crouches close to the head of the sleeping girl, seeming to watch over her. In the foreground of the picture is the crane that personifies the idea of judgment.

To the left of the crane are a bunch of purple grapes, a plate of cakes, and a bowl of roses topped by the model of a centaur.

JUDGEMENT AND THE CRANE

Fossil records give us evidence that the crane is one of the oldest surviving birds, having remained relatively unchanged for ten million years. It's impossible for us to have a full comprehension of just what this means, but it's one of the reasons why the crane is the bird of Judgement, aspects of which are longevity and rebirth. Traditional interpretations of this card often show people rising from their graves, defying mortality. In Japan, people practiced a particular breathing technique, emulating the cranes which they believed lived for the thousand years. Also, crane eggs were added to a magical tincture that was believed to confer immortality. In other Eastern countries the elegant dance of the crane was seen as the epitome of the power of flight – and flight meant access to the Gods – and was copied using long stilts. Because of their great age, cranes also represent wisdom.

Curiously, the crane is strongly linked to both the power of speech and the ability to render sounds as symbols. One of the most intriguing stories about the crane is that this is the bird whose flight pattern inspired the God, Hermes/Mercury, to invent the alphabet. This is why, in Northern Europe, the crane belongs to this God. An alphabet isn't just a series of letters that depict sounds, but each shape holds an entire world of mysteries within it; concepts that still speak of the concerns of the ancient peoples who invented them. The Bambara in Africa believe that the crane was present at the birth of speech itself, and secret ceremonies of initiation talk of the crane that first said, "I speak."

In Celtic lore, the crane – or heron – is one of the most meaningful and sacred of all birds. We can always recognize power animals in that it is forbidden to eat their flesh, and this taboo goes for the crane. Here too there's an association with language; "Crane Knowledge" meant the understanding of the ancient tree alphabet, or Ogham. Here, the crane figure is an aspect of the hag goddess or Cailleach.

In the Buddhist Crane Ceremony that took place in the eleventh century, the names of warriors slain in battle were attached to the legs of cranes. The cranes were then released to carry the spirits of these warriors back home to their Gods.

Significance of Judgement and the Crane

The girl in the card here appears to be comatose; maybe she's intoxicated. She seems to be drifting down a river of some kind – this represents the river of the Underworld. The rowan tree – sacred to the Druids as the tree of rebirth and resurrection – has fruits hanging in it which carry the same symbolism as the tree.

Rebirth is connected with death, but as we've seen with the Death card, this is nothing to do with the shut-down of the physical body. All the travails of the cards that precede Judgement combine to make the sum total of their parts, and the renewal implied here is the dawning of a new kind of creative energy. Liberation often comes after a period of difficulty; this is over. When we pull back the string of a bow, the energy stored in the cord, once released, propels the arrow. Drawing this card means that you are now prepared to be that arrow; you are refreshed, invigorated, and now it's time to fly as you find confidence in all your abilities, skills and – yes – attractiveness. The only judgement that you need to make is for yourself and of yourself, but in order to do this lucidly, it's a good idea to talk to close friends and companions. When anything is possible, there are choices to be made; you might be in such a position, and it's important that you make the next step with clarity of thought, with the sharpness of intellect (the alphabet, inspired by the sharp wings of the crane against a crisp sky, is a good image to remind you of this) rather than the angst of emotion. You also need be confident that so long as you remain dispassionate about your next move, it is part of a momentous pattern of spiritual awakening that has been germinating for some time; you are a bud about to burst into a flower, a fruit that is coming into ripeness. This card is also the potential for new beginnings in the form of new life, and this might be something that is part of the decision that you are faced with. Whatever you believe about "karma," it's true that our ability to make free choices is a part of the karmic process, and you can be confident that whatever you do will bring you to exactly where you need to be.

JUDGEMENT REVERSED

All the tools you need are laid out before you. You know inherently that whatever you do will be right, but nevertheless, something seems to be stopping you. It might be time to take a leap in the dark, to make almost any decision rather than stay in a stagnant state. If you don't water a plant, it dies. The only "wrong" thing you can do is fizzle into a melancholic state of non-movement. Even one small step – changing one single deep-rooted habit – will help you in your forward trajectory. What have you got to lose?

21
THE WORLD

Il Mondo

The Hoopoe

"We should not pretend to judge the World only by the intellect."
~Carl Gustav Jung

KEYWORDS
Completion, fulfillment, perfection, expansion of horizons, synthesis, success, admiration, achievement

DESCRIPTION
A young woman, with dusky blue skin and dark hair, sits in the foreground of the picture. The woman wears a red blouse and is crowned with laurels. She is holding the bird that personifies the ideals of this card, The Hoopoe.

Behind her is the Planet Earth, divided into ten segments, like a globe. The woman looks towards the globe.

In the top left hand corner of the picture, peeking over the globe, is a small cherubic character. At the other side appears the head and wing of an eagle.

Hovering to the right of the globe is a small, winged lion-like creature.

The World and the Hoopoe

This is an unusual bird, with a questioning look and a distinctive "crown" of feathers upon its head. Its curious name is derived from its call, a distinctive, mellow "hoop hoop" sound.

The hoopoe, for a long time considered to be a magical and mysterious bird as evidenced by its appearance on the walls of tombs in ancient Egypt and Greece, plays the starring role in a remarkable allegorical tale by twelfth-century Sufi poet Farid Ud Din Attar. It's because of this tale that the Hoopoe is the bird belonging to The World. In this story, called "The Conference of the Birds," the entire population of birds decides to undertake a pilgrimage to find their particular deity king, a mysterious bird called the Simurgh. The birds have to undertake many struggles, squabbles and upsets along the way, much like our journey through the tarot. Some of them even make excuses and drop out altogether. However, throughout the entire journey the birds are unified by the wisdom and diplomatic skills of the Hoopoe who takes on the role of leader, providing guidance and encouragement. It's evident from the word "Bismillah" that's etched upon his beak that the Hoopoe has an important spiritual vocation within the story. At the end of the journey they realize that they, collectively, are the Simurgh; they are the God that they have been seeking.

The Significance of The World and the Hoopoe

As the last card of the Major Arcana, The World signifies the end of the journey, completion and fulfillment. The character here is sitting down, relaxing, a wistful look on her face. She knows that, for now, her tasks are ended and that the rewards of her efforts are reaped, and the laurel wreath that crowns her head is evidence that she's victorious. The hoopoe sits comfortably in her lap; she is the sum total of all the other cards, secure, content, knows that she is the divinity she has been seeking.

However, The World continues to turn. There's never any real "ending," and even after death the ripples of a life continue to affect people and events, sometimes even more meaningfully than during their life. We can understand intellectually that every single thing on the planet is linked, but here we have full emotional integration, too. When this happens, there's no turning back. For example, once we completely understand the adverse effects certain substances or practices can have on ourselves or on the planet, our lives can change as we know that we have to address these issues, that both the problem and the solution are in our hands. We can't wait for other people or the Government to take the lead. There's a Buddhist tenet: "be, do, have." This short phrase is the essence of cause and effect, very appropriate if you have drawn this card. Be who you are, do what you need to do, and you will, by default, have everything you need. Again, this is an interesting philosophy that has now become a living reality, enriching your life and influencing the people around you as they recognize the inner power that generates your outer shine.

The World, too, is understanding, generous, and all-encompassing. Here, you realize the true understanding of forgiveness is that there really is nothing to forgive, that everything had its reason and purpose however incomprehensible things might have seemed at the time. The meaning of trust, too, suddenly becomes very clear, and this renders everything very exciting, because now anything is possible. Learning to trust is like learning to ice-skate, knowing the nature of the blade on the ice and the balance that comes in between as the operable part of the equation. Suddenly, everything becomes light, not heavy, and as the world opens up we accept the possibility of the impossible. If you take away the commonly accepted beliefs about how long an hour is, or how many of them make up a day, then it's even possible that the universe was indeed constructed in seven days.

THE WORLD REVERSED

If there's anything you feel that you've left undone, or left unsaid, now is the time to say it. This requires a great deal of courage, but the alternative – not dealing with it – will only lead to anguish and regret. There may be things about you that have been held up to a mirror, habits so ingrained that you had no longer even thought about them. This is an opportunity, but you need to act in full consciousness to turn things around. You'll be very glad you did.

THE FOUR FLOCKS OF THE MINOR ARCANA
(CUPS, WANDS, SWORDS, AND COINS)

It always seems to be somehow disrespectful to refer to these fifty six cards as "minor;" however, it's true to say that they do tend to play a supporting role to the real stars of the show, the twenty-two cards of the Major Arcana.

Here, the Minor Arcana are divided into four flocks of birds. Each suit has a specific bird assigned to it which reflects the element that rules over that suit.

From the North, the element of earth, flies the tiny wren who carries a coin in its beak.

From the South and the element of fire, we see the skylark, symbolizing Wands.

From the East, carried along by the element of air, is the seagull, representing Swords.

And finally from the West the kingfisher signifies the element of water and the suit of cups.

The final four cards of each "flock" straddle the transition from birds to human kind, and accordingly these cards feature people; a Queen and a King, and then a God and a Goddess. The God and Goddess cards have shapeshifting abilities, and so the birds on these cards transport us to fantastical realms.

You'll notice that each of the first ten cards in each suit ask a question. This question is meant to trigger thoughts, ideas, conversation, maybe even possible solutions.

If you are using the minor arcane as a way of giving a quick one-card reading, use the question posed by the card as a catalyst to help look at something in a different light.

THE SUIT OF CUPS
COPPE

THE ELEMENT OF WATER REPRESENTED BY THE KINGFISHER

The suit of cups is all about emotions and relationships, moods and feelings, matters of the heart (in fact, in "normal" decks of playing cards, the suit of cups has been transformed, very appropriately, into the suit of hearts).

For the purposes of this deck, the kingfisher has been chosen to collectively personify the notion of cups, and this is because of a Greek myth. The Halcyon Birds were a husband and wife, Ceyx, the King of Trachis, and Halcyone, the daughter of the Lord of the Winds, Aeolus. Passionately in love, Ceyx and Halcyone were reunited as kingfishers after their deaths. Kingfishers are able to nest on water. And the Halcyon Days that we sometimes talk of actually refer to the period of calm in the middle of winter when the weather grows calmer for a while and hints at a promise of the summer to look forward to.

Cards belonging to this suit relate to people that are emotional and passionate, wear their hearts on their sleeves, and whose moods, more than others, are affected by the weather and the phases of the moon. Cups people are liable to say exactly what they're feeling, sometimes to the consternation of those around them. Where they appear prominently in a spread, be aware that feelings and emotions run high and that the rational, thinking mind is likely to be overridden. Sometimes, no matter how we try to rationalize things, we simply can't dismiss our intuitive side, even though we might not know precisely where we are being taken, or how.

The final four cards of this suit sees our flock of kingfishers shape shifting into human characters, the King and Queen and God and Goddess of cups.

I
THE ACE OF CUPS

KEYWORDS
New ideas, growth and possibilities. Inspiration, intuition and lucky "hunches," powerful feelings.

QUESTION INSPIRED BY THIS CARD:
WHAT CAN MAKE ME HAPPY?

DRAWN UPRIGHT

The Ace of Cups is all about the emotional impact of new beginnings. The lone kingfisher could herald a new love, a new realization, a new idea, or perhaps the dawning of an understanding and recognition of a new dimension to your own feelings and personality. It could signify the same in a partner or other close person.

Sometimes, a new realization is brought about by the end of something; for example, the end of a relationship can bring with it a feeling of optimism, freedom, and infinite possibilities. The Ace of Cups, therefore, can signify something good being born of something bad. The lone kingfisher that depicts this card can be overwhelmed by the input of new feelings and needs to find a way of dealing with them; meditation might help. The realization that you can be happy in your own skin is one of the lessons being taught, too. Sometimes, this card can herald a physical birth as well as a figurative one.

The potential for growth and learning is profound, and is in your own hands.

DRAWN REVERSED

Sometimes we can be swamped with emotion to the point that we cease to be able to operate effectively in everyday matters. When we're at the mercy of our feelings in this way, we tend to lack both stability and perspective. It's important to regain some of this perspective in a particularly emotionally-charged matter. Sometimes other peoples' demands can drain us of any energy and we don't realize this is happening until we're able to extricate ourselves from the situation/relationship. It would be a good time to take some time away, to see a figurative new horizon so as to see the metaphorical bigger picture. Then, all the inspiration that you thought had dried up will begin to return. You need emotional replenishment.

II
TWO OF CUPS

Keywords
Harmony, love, partnerships. High emotional charge, sex.

Question inspired by this card:
What is it in another person that makes me happy?

Drawn Upright

The two kingfishers here indicate love between two people. In particular, this card signifies love in the erotic and amorous sense, but can indicate a close working partnership too, perhaps a creative endeavor in which the emotions run high. The two kingfishers shown here may symbolize the thrill of a new relationship, or a finding that there's a new dimension to an existing one that lends it an even deeper meaning. The harmony of two people on an equal emotional footing means that the situation can be tempestuous from time to time as both partners are equally passionate and strong-willed. Wherever emotions are close to the surface between two people, battles and arguments can ensue; this is a healthy part of a passionate interplay between equals and of course the making-up is a delightful part of the equation!

Drawn Reversed

Whatever the nature of the relationship, there are times when we simply don't see eye-to-eye with a partner. When we're out of synch with one another, we can become exasperated and annoyed. Close partnerships require a great deal of compromise; for gains and sacrifices to be truly equal needs both partners to be careful that they neither give away too much, nor demand too little. It might be time to take an objective overview rather than let the heat of emotions fan the flames of discord. It takes courage to recognize this sort of necessity, but a part of you knows that this makes sense. After all, if the relationship *is* important it will withstand any tests, including that of separation. If it isn't, then it's better to find out sooner rather than later. Cups belong to the element of water and the moon, so gain perspective by thinking of how different things were, say, two months ago, and know that they will be different again two months hence.

III
THREE OF CUPS

KEYWORDS
Celebrations, happiness, family occasions, promotions.

QUESTION INSPIRED BY THIS CARD:
WHY DO I NEED AN EXCUSE TO HAVE A PARTY?

DRAWN UPRIGHT

The three kingfishers here are enjoying a party; it might be that your life has suddenly turned into a social whirlwind. Enjoy it! It's definitely time for celebrations, meeting new people and making new friends, as well as taking care of the old ones. Indeed, sometimes we can neglect our oldest friends simply because the friendship is so easy that we can take one another for granted; this card might inspire you to re-establish contact with someone, or they might seek you out for a specific reason; a birthday, wedding, or christening. A house-warming might be in the offing, too. However, life is too short to always need such a reason for a get-together, and the more formal the occasion the more difficult it can be to catch up properly. You might decide to throw your own party for a few of your closest friends, or arrange a get-together that's under your own terms.

Drawn Reversed

A hectic social life can be fabulous, but can also be draining, especially if you're burning the candle at both ends for any significant period of time. Continual partying is tiring, and you might be asking yourself, what's the point of a constant clamor of new faces and names, especially if the circumstances aren't right to meet someone with whom there's a significant connection? It's time to spend a few evenings indoors. Replenish your energy and find perspective in your social life; be more discerning about who you spend your valuable time with.

IV
Four of Cups

Keywords
Being in the doldrums; stagnation, boredom, depression, fear of being alone.

Question Inspired by This Card:
What Do I Learn from Boredom?

Drawn Upright
If the kingfisher nests on the sea, on open water that moves and changes constantly, then this card is the opposite, and akin to the unmoving waters of a murky lake. You might be stuck in a rut as far as a close relationship is concerned, and you're struggling to be able to change matters in any direction, either for better or worse. But don't worry; this feeling of stagnation is part of the process which will ultimately trigger change. Then again, this fallow period may belong to another aspect of your life. Again, try to see this time for what it is; a watershed. To gain a sense of perspective you might decide to enjoy such a "dull" time and concentrate on all those little things you've being putting off doing; boring and tedious, maybe, but they will give you a sense of achievement in the meantime.

Drawn Reversed
You might find yourself in a sudden rush of changes; these could present as the possibility of a new relationship or as a series of highly-charged emotions that energize and enliven. Such heady and turbulent feelings and changes can be unsettling but you also know that this has been a long time coming! Your world may be feeling unstable, but again, you must realize that this is a necessary part of a process. Try to establish even a small routine, something that is an everyday anchor in an excitingly stormy sea, whilst at the same time allowing yourself to be carried in the current, safe in the knowledge that the ultimate security is in trusting in the Universe.

V
Five of Cups

Keywords
Shattered dreams; a feeling of loss; opening up old wounds; cautious hope.

Question inspired by this card: How do I enrich my own life?

Drawn Upright

The five kingfishers here signify the loss we feel when we realize that a dream has been shattered. We need time to grieve and to reflect about what happened, and when we're in such a state of mind it's usually difficult to see the way ahead. But it's important not to dismiss the need to process properly what's happened. It could be that the nature of a relationship has changed and you need to come to terms with the fall-out that this causes. Try to lift yourself out of the depression by thinking of the old adage "it's better to have loved and lost than never to have loved at all." And make a list of all the good things in your life, rather than concentrating on the things that you don't have. It's also easy to react to what's happened by rushing into something new to try to fill the hole in your life; tread with caution at this time because your judgment is likely to be unreliable right now.

DRAWN REVERSED

There's the possibility of someone coming back into your life, the chance of a reunion or a new start. However, this will only become a reality if you have truly learned the lessons of the past and are dispassionate enough to be able to apply them constructively as lessons that you've learned. You have all the information to hand, so you can actually make a rational choice. Beware the temptation to rush headlong into something during a moment of loneliness or weakness; make sure that your life has enough infrastructure in it to make you strong, and you'll make the right choice.

VI
SIX OF CUPS

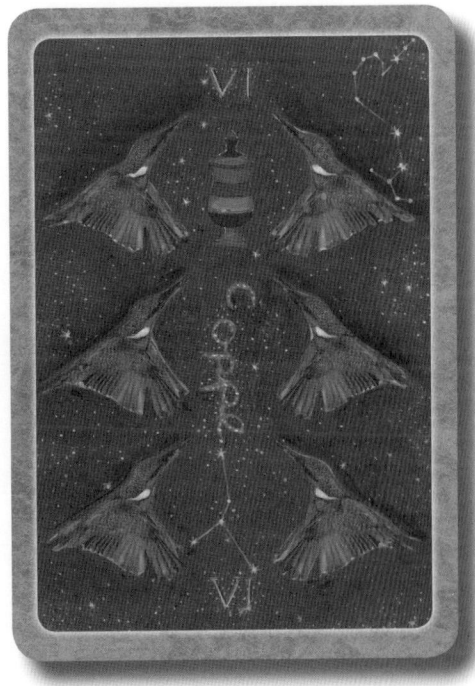

KEYWORDS
Learning from the past; nostalgia and happy memories; karmic rewards; contentment.

QUESTION INSPIRED BY THIS CARD: HOW CAN I LEARN FROM THE PAST?

DRAWN UPRIGHT

There are six birds here, and six is the number of harmony and balance. It's time for everything in the past to be looked at with affection, to effect reconciliation that will pave the future with emotional success and satisfaction. It's only with the perspective of time and distance that we can truly learn from what's happened in the past, and this is the time to do so. You have also realized that it's not good to rush into something new, too soon.

If you've ever told anyone you loved them, then these words resonate forever and contribute to making the world a better place. You are glad that such positive feelings are a part of your life, and that the past is fully integrated. These relationships might involve lovers or old friends, or even that you had once thought were enemies.

DRAWN REVERSED

It's good to look back at the past as part of our journey and also to project forward into the future using the lessons learned – but it's also vitally important to be in the here and now. If we dwell too much in the past then we can effectively block forward progress. You might find it easier to understand the things that have happened, any repeating patterns, with the help of a therapist or a neutral confidante. It's also sometimes easy to either paint a rosier picture of the past than is accurate, or to do the opposite and cut off old ties completely. But don't throw out the baby with the bath water, since this is something that you might regret in the future. Be kind to yourself, and live in the moment.

VII
SEVEN OF CUPS

KEYWORDS
Illusions and mirage; fool's gold; emotional temptation and the need for objectivity.

QUESTION INSPIRED BY THIS CARD:
WHAT REALLY MATTERS TO ME?

DRAWN UPRIGHT

This is a time when amazing possibilities are being paraded before you. However, you need to be careful that you're not dazzled by the possibility of such glittering potential and that you retain objectivity. It might be tempting to grab at everything that's offered, but right now you need to step back and wait to see what floats to the surface and will bear the close scrutiny of the sunshine, and what sinks to the murky depths below. This might be regarding a choice of suitors; if you can't make that choice, it could be that none of them are right. Don't be too quick to take action or try to stick butterflies with pins. Be patient, and enjoy the process, since right now you are able to gain a real understanding of the nature of illusion, or Maya. The right choice will become more concrete and obvious if you give it a little time, and in the meantime fix your life with solid, real things. Simple things, such as making sure that you are eating properly. Gardening, cleaning, having a clear-out; these real, everyday routines will help you gain a sense of perspective.

Drawn Reversed

Reality can be obfuscated by many things; living in the past, fantasizing about the future, maybe even relying on drugs or alcohol. It can take a wrench to clamber out of such habits, but it's important that you do so. Sometimes we use a relationship to paste over the reality of our lives, afraid to spend time alone to really examine what's under our noses. Conversely, meditation and contemplation are all very well and have their correct time and place, but too much navel-gazing is as bad as none at all. There's always a time and a place for fantasy and the world of the imagination, but too much time spent in dreams is unhealthy and imbalanced. See the seven birds here as two pairs of three, balanced by the axle of the seventh bird in the centre. You have it in you to find that balance.

VIII
Eight of Cups

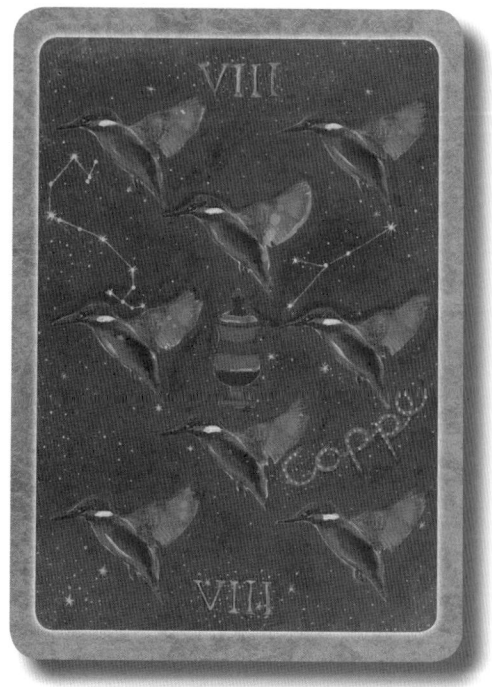

Keywords

Moving on, changing a relationship, seeing the bigger picture.

Question inspired by this card:
Who is the most important person in my life?

Drawn Upright

Sometimes, there's no choice but to leave a relationship, and no matter what it's nature, this is tough. Initially, there needs to be a process of total severance and separation; distance is needed for perspective. The eight birds here tell you that you are strong enough and have the courage to do this. It can be hard to let go of old patterns of behavior even though they might have made us miserable; such unhappiness can become a habit, a part of our life, and it can take time for us to realize that we'd forgotten what "happy" even meant! Now is the time for you to face the possibility of such a positive "bereavement," to look at the meaning of your life and to address concerns which have remained dormant, masked by extraneous matters. This might be a good time to take a journey somewhere to help get some sense of perspective; bear in mind, though, that you can't escape yourself and your own emotions. Accept the way you're feeling.

Drawn Reversed

When we are in grief or pain after a separation, it can be tempting to shut yourself away from friends and the people who can give you support. And it can be easy to divide up friends between ex-partners; there's no need to do this. You can be a friend and give support and guidance to others as well as taking comfort from your own friends. Don't cut yourself off! In time it will be easy to pick out the good things and discard the rest. If you are feeling emotionally shattered, exhausted or drained, do all the little things that make you happy and will help you to heal.

IX
Nine of Cups

Keywords
Happiness and joy, well-being and fulfillment, and yet also wanting more.

Question inspired by this card:
How can I be happy in the moment?

Drawn Upright

Dreams and wishes come true, and there's a feeling of happiness, abundance, good fortune. Something that you might have been working on for a long time has come to fruition, a relationship is at a very good stage, and all the joys of the world are upon you! It should be time to celebrate and relax, and indeed you're doing this, but there's still a niggling feeling that something is missing. Maybe something remains unsaid, or you feel churlish to admit the possibility that something isn't quite right in view of all the good things that you know are in your life. Comparing yourself to others and being grateful for what you have is one thing, but this isn't necessarily constructive. For the time being, put any doubt or fears to one side and enjoy this moment and these times. Relish the benefits of all the hard mental, physical, and emotional work that you have put into constructing your own happy life.

Drawn Reversed

When we're comfortable, it can be easy to take things for granted, to forget about the hard times or any previous moments of emotional difficulty, loneliness, and confusion. You are in a good place right now, but remember that you have to take care of the structure of your life in order to maintain balance. Count your blessings and perhaps put some time into helping those less fortunate than yourself. If we choose to see all the things that we don't have, we'll never be happy; make it your mission to regard yourself as unique, and go back to that child-like state of astonishment at what a beautiful planet this is!

X
Ten of Cups

KEYWORDS
Everything you always wanted; abundance, a happy home and family life, success in all things.

QUESTION INSPIRED BY THIS CARD:
HOW CAN I SHARE MY HAPPINESS?

DRAWN UPRIGHT
These ten kingfishers tell you that dreams can come true! Relationships can be wonderful and all the things you ever wanted are here, available, now. The word "abundance" is used a lot these days, but as far as this card is concerned it's extremely apt. Life is abundant. Your own joy and happiness extends to everyone around you; these cups are, literally, overflowing! You're rewarded for all the hard work, struggles, and tribulations that the preceding nine cards tell the story of. You are at the pinnacle of success, happiness, and satisfaction.

DRAWN REVERSED
Shifting sands; you feel insecure, as though all the things that are most precious to you are on the brink of slipping away. However, fears are always much worse when they are left unexpressed, so talk to someone about your concerns rather than trying to handle everything all on your own. It's possible that you're having sleepless nights because of all the worry, but a clinical step-by-step approach in the clear light of day will help you to gain perspective. Nothing is insurmountable! And there's nothing to fear except fear itself. You need to find the common ground with a person close to you and not get caught up in miniscule details which really don't matter in the great scheme of things.

XI
Queen of Cups

"It's not the having, it's the getting."
~Elizabeth Taylor

Keywords
Gentle; sensitive; loving; dreamy.

Description
A beautiful young woman, wearing a white swan-like dress, gazes dreamily into the left of the picture. The violet-blue night background matches perfectly the color of her eyes. The constellations in the skies behind her match the constellations of diamonds which adore her both as jeweler and as sparkles in her dress. There are two kingfishers with her.

Drawn Upright
This is a young woman with her heart on her sleeve. Dreamy and affectionate, she is tender, emotional, gentle, and full of love for everything in the beautiful world she finds herself surrounded by; people, animals, even plants, trees, and cloud formations do not escape her all-embracing delight. Creative and

expressive, sometimes her creativity will take the form of something solid – perhaps she's a painter or sculptor – or it could be that she is a singer or musician. Deeply sensitive, it's as well for those around the Queen of Cups to realize that such sensitivity can sometimes make the world a difficult place to deal with, especially in one so open. Some discreet protection might be necessary lest this little Queen takes on board too many of other peoples' problems, since she can become battered and drained by them. Her own empathy can be in many ways a double-edged sword; she can see the beauty in all things, even in the most divisive or dangerous of people. The Queen of Cups would find it useful to practice some form of psychic protection as a matter of course, and needs to be aware that such wonderful openness can leave her exposed – although she should never try to "toughen up" or change her child-like demeanor. Her charm means that many find her utterly captivating.

DRAWN REVERSED

Delusional; disconnected; possible mental health issues.

Such a dreamy, sensitive nature, without any kind of channeling, can mean that this Queen can be confused, indecisive, ineffectual. Unable to define her place in the world if she has no way to manifest her more imaginative dreams, she can become disillusioned, disappointed, drifting in a world with nothing to steer her course. Any practice which requires some kind of self-discipline, such as yoga, or indeed training in almost anything that interests her, would be beneficial. However the Queen of Swords, reversed, lacks the necessary impetus to bring such an influence into her life, and may well need outside help. Too much time on her own can give her strange delusions and she may be prone to acting out different roles with different people.

XII
THE KING OF CUPS

"I hold a beast, an angel, and a madman in me, and my enquiry is as to their working, and my problem is their subjugation and victory, downthrow and upheaval, and my effort is their self-expression."

~Dylan Thomas

KEYWORDS
Idealistic; romantic; ambitious; dreamy; creative.

DESCRIPTION
A young man gazes back earnestly at the viewer, a friendly look on his face; he's young, optimistic, full of dreams and ideas, his mind ripe with imagination. On his left lapel is the symbol of Scorpio, one of the three astrological signs that are ruled by the water element. There's one kingfisher in the painting, and the young man stands before a starry sky, the planet earth hanging to the left of the picture.

DRAWN UPRIGHT
A tender-hearted man, the King of Cups is so idealistic that, wherever possible, he will follow his dreams and try to make them come true. A creature

of impulse, he will drop anything and go off in pursuit of an idea that captures his imagination. This is the sort of person who would have followed Christ, or gone on the Grail Quest – the more obscure or metaphysical the object of his search, the more fascinated and inspired he is likely to be. In fact, his imagination is fired even further with the romantic idealism of an almost-impossible task!

This card tells of the possibility of a new romantic attachment, and also serves as a reminder of the necessity for "grounding," that the head and the heart should operate concordantly in an ideal world. There are problems in "real life" that this young man will face with a great deal of velour, but not always with an equable amount of common sense. This trait, however, can be one of his most charming features, and he does tend to bring out protective powers in the females that surround him. The King of Cups in many ways does need to be protected from the "real" world and has a tendency to do this by using his imagination as a sort of barrier; the result is that in so doing he will often make that world a more beautiful place.

DRAWN REVERSED

Delusion; fantasy; drugs, drink and other techniques of avoidance or escapism.

All the dreamy idealism of this King, when reversed, becomes soured as the harshness of the real world impinges, and when his constant striving for the impossible and the idealistic may result in disappointment and disillusion. This means that the King of Cups can become deluded as he strives to retain his own sense of what's genuine in a world that seems to him to be more and more hostile. This isn't the truth, of course, but an illusion due to an illogical way of thinking which has no counter balance in reality. This character, without outside help or any kind of trigger for a revelation of self-awareness, can become a sad person, lost in his own mind's eye, happier to occupy his own version of reality rather than stepping out to encompass the very beautiful real world that lies just beyond his peripheral vision. Drugs and drink can also help to reinforce this deluded belief, so if this card is drawn, it's worth taking this into consideration.

God and Goddess of Cups

XIII
God of Cups

The final pair of cards in the suit of Cups takes as its bird the Feng Huang, the mysterious Chinese equivalent of the phoenix. Unlike the phoenix, however, the Feng Huang comprises two birds that live together as a pair, symbolizing the union of opposites, male and female, light and dark, yin and yang.

The Feng Huang lives in a magical Kingdom somewhere East of China, in the place where the Sun rises; sometimes the bird is seen with a cup of golden fire. The bird itself flies across the skies carrying all the Universe in its wake.

"For man, as for flower and beast and bird, the supreme triumph is to be most vividly, most perfectly alive."

~D.H. Lawrence

KEYWORDS
Charming; intuitive; emotional.

DESCRIPTION
A handsome young Asian man, crowned as befits his God-like status, holds aloft the mythical bird, the Feng Huang, whose golden wings are outstretched. This oriental firebird is also depicted on his sleeve.

DRAWN UPRIGHT
Of all the Gods, the God of Cups is the one who is most in touch with his feminine side. This can sometimes be disconcerting to others who will find him an enigmatic and sometimes mysterious character. Sensitive and artistic, the God of Cups is likely to have made a creative career for himself, since he is able to manifest his dreams in the real world. He is inspired by a deep love of nature and humanity, and although he is liable to have been hurt in his earlier life, in later years this God will have learned to separate his love for humanity from the very real problems that people have, and no longer takes thing personally. The God of Cups makes for a good counselor, combining thoughtfulness and empathy with a streak of practicality which makes for good advice.

The God of Cups feels things very deeply, and will sometimes have to remove himself, mentally if not physically, from scenes of conflict. He is, however, a passionate and demanding person where it comes to affairs of the heart; in his early years he may not realize that this moody intensity can be off-putting to people!

DRAWN REVERSED
A fantasist; addictive personality; obsessive.

All the passion and empathy of this God, when reversed, can take the dark side of his moods and emphasize them over the light. In which case we find someone that finds it difficult to deal with the world, and will be inclined to find his way in it by drifting rather than making any firm plans. So open to outside influences, it takes little for this reversed God to be caught up in the unhealthier side of life; drugs and drink, for example, or for him to be influenced by unsavory people. He can also be prone to very deep bouts of depression which he may not even realize he's suffering from, and since he doesn't really trust anyone, this could well affect his future happiness. Since he can easily alienate people, this King can have a lonely life, and if anyone comes into his field of vision he is likely to become obsessive. He needs to find some meaning in his life – preferably in a sense of self-worth.

XIV
GODDESS OF CUPS

"I never saw a wild thing sorry for itself. A small bird will drop frozen dead from a bough without ever having felt sorry for itself."
~D. H. Lawrence

KEYWORDS

Femininity; nurturing; compassion; intuition.

DESCRIPTION

A beautiful young Asian woman, dressed in gold and red and wearing an elaborate crown, sits astride the Feng Huang, the mythical Chinese firebird that is her familiar. She looks directly at the viewer, firmly holding on to the symbol of the Cup. The background of the picture is royal blue and is spangled with stars.

DRAWN UPRIGHT

As the Goddess who rules over the element of cups (which in turn represents water and the epitome of the feminine aspect) the Goddess of Cups also signifies the feminine absolute: the Mother, the daughter, the sister. She encompasses all the nurturing qualities of the female, and all the capricious ones, too. This is a creative, artistic woman with an air of mystery, befitting in one who's so closely aligned to all the occult knowledge of the moon as it provides a nocturnal mirror for the Sun. The Goddess of Cups is remarkably self-contained, unafraid to express her emotions. Despite her powerful nurturing tendencies, doesn't feel the need to please others for the sake of pleasing alone, a quality which does seem to be peculiar to many motherly types; not so with this Goddess. A powerful woman, the Goddess of Cups has a powerful imagination and intuition, but is also able to bring forth these dreams and ideas into the material world; she can manifest them in ways that can sometimes affect many people. She is able to use any emotional trauma almost as "material," turning it to something useful and effective. Something of a drama queen, this Goddess likes to turn heads and make people think.

Drawn Reversed

Manipulative; dependent; depressed.

Reversed, the Goddess of Cups can be moody and difficult, wielding her emotions like a club and using them – whether real or imagined – to punish those close to her. Her nerves are constantly on edge, and this woman might have a history of nervous collapse or breakdowns. Subsequently, she might have learned that this is a good survival mechanism that can enable her to get what she wants, and she might become highly manipulative as a result, using her highs and lows to affect everyone in her life. When stuck in this role, her many talents remain unused, when really the best therapy would be for her to stop gazing internally, embrace the world and do something that will take her out of her own self-obsession; helping others in some small way, for example. It's easy for the reversed Goddess of Cups to be the sort of mother who's "sacrifices" make her a "martyr."

THE SUIT OF WANDS
BASTONI
THE ELEMENT OF FIRE REPRESENTED BY THE SKYLARK

The suit of wands is all about the warmth and dynamism, intuitive spirituality and the inspiration of the fire element. The wand is an appropriate symbol; think of sparks of magic coming from the end of it, like flames.

For the purposes of this particular deck, the skylark has been chosen to represent the notion of wands. This is because of the exuberant and unexpected way that this little bird leaps from the ground and into the sky, very much like a burst of flame. Robert Graves, in *The White Goddess*, writes of how the skylark. "...flies singing up to adore him," meaning the Sun. The wand also stands for the process of intuition and inspiration, and the process of tuning in to the subconscious.

Cards belonging to this suit relate to people who are spiritual and inspirational, and are creatively driven by both internal and external factors. These people are liable to be curious about the workings of the psyche, interested in esoteric ways of processing thoughts, events, and other factors in their lives. Lateral thinkers, Wands people will bend the rules without actually breaking them and will find magical nuggets of interest and wonder in the most insignificant things around them. Because there's a powerful streak of childlike imagination and an ability to find fun in any situation, you'll often find that Wands people are surrounded by children of all ages.

The final four cards of this suit see the skylark flocks shapeshifting into human beings. These are the King and Queen of Wands, and the God and Goddess of Wands.

I
THE ACE OF WANDS

Keywords
Creation, initiative, inspiration; the first spark that lights the flame

Question inspired by this card:
What inspires me?

Drawn Upright
An idea, started in the mind by a burst of inspired thought, has the potential to be made real and manifest in the material world as well as in the world of spirit that engenders it. The skylark that belongs to the ace of wands is an exciting bird. Here, she tells us that the ambition and optimism that you need to make something "real" are all at your disposal. Yes, there will be hard work – but you know exactly what it is you need to do, and the work will be accomplished almost like a forest fire – speedily and efficiently, driven by an inspiration that has divine sources. You have great levels of enthusiasm that will inspire anyone involved in this idea.

Drawn Reversed
You need to look at the reasons that there may be blocks, not necessarily in your creative ideas, but in your ability to manifest them. Drawing this card says that such obstacles might not be due to external factors, but to internal ones, although you might be blaming things outside of yourself! This state of frustration can affect other things in our lives too; sex drive, for example, can be dampened as we cast around for blame and sometimes heap it squarely on the head of the person closest to us. The seeming inability to manifest your ideas can make you feel flat and dull, but the trick here is to remember that this is all a part of the process...and to relax. Be patient; like all things, this will pass.

II
Two of Wands

Keywords
Productive partnerships of all kinds. A good working relationship, inspired communications.

Question inspired by this card:
How do I share my ideas?

Drawn Upright

Think of the kingfishers on this card as alchemists of transformation, a reminder that two heads can be better than one. Having said this, it can sometimes be difficult to have a really good productive partnership with someone, whatever form that partnership might take. This card tells you that this elusive partnership is possible, and at hand. All creative partnerships involve a level of honesty and a relinquishing of some aspects of control and mutual trust and a willingness to override the ego which might initially seem to be a pretty scary prospect. But in fact the level of freedom and liberation that the sharing of ideas can bring means that the way is cleared for true creativity and communication to flow, and leaves open the possibility for a lone idea to suddenly become much bigger than the sum of its parts. This rule applies to schemes both modest and grand. Even an honest heart-to-heart conversation is a sort of dance, an interaction of energies and intention to make something else.

Drawn Reversed

A close working relationship can be tense as both partners struggle to have their thoughts take precedent, especially if both parties are equally passionate or if both are equally unwilling to be flexible about their vision. Flare-ups and arguments can ensue, and the end objective can move out of sight, can even become embroiled in tiresome legalities. Flexibility might be required on both sides, but neither partner is able to give in. A compromise between creativity and cash might also cause friction! Maybe a third party needs to help arbitrate, to get back to the primary objective and to see not only the true cause of the conflict, but to see where there's agreement and to concentrate on this. This card tells you that it's not too late to save the situation provided both parties are willing to do so.

III
Three of Wands

KEYWORDS

Opportunities, planning, fusion, travel, culmination of past efforts and relationships.

QUESTION INSPIRED BY THIS CARD:
HOW DOES AN IDEA TRANSFORM INTO REALITY?

DRAWN UPRIGHT

The three birds here tell us that there are many opportunities in the offing. You need to be aware that some of these opportunities will be exactly what you need, others may seem oblique – but regard all of them with an open mind. They might be related to your career, or to financial matters, or perhaps expansion in all directions. One particular opportunity may also be related to a creative idea that you've been working on for a long time. The chance for travel comes with this card, too; this could be related to the venture you've been working on or might appear to be totally unrelated but which would have benefits in areas as yet unforeseen. Your mind is focused, you are clear about what you need to do next, and all the help you need, whatever form it takes, makes itself available.

DRAWN REVERSED

Sometimes when there's too much choice it can be overwhelming and we end up doing nothing at all. In this case, everything can go by the wayside; faced with the actual possibility of dreams becoming realities can seem too good to be true and we become frozen, like a rabbit in the headlights. There is a chance here to grasp an opportunity, something that's been a long time coming, but for some reason you seem to want to sabotage it. It's not too late to pull it from the brink, but you really need to focus hard and think clearly; then take action! This action might be to say that the time isn't right for this particular dream; so long as your reasons for this are clear and not born of fear or laziness, then the opportunity will re-present itself. It's a matter of trusting that good things *can* happen, and that you deserve them to.

IV
Four of Wands

Keywords
Hearth and home; security, comfort and stability. Reaping the rewards of effort.

Question inspired by this card:
What do I really need?

Drawn Upright

The home and family can create a stable environment from which to go out and conquer the world. You have made this possibility for yourself, whether in the traditional manner or in the strength and faithfulness of the friends that surround you, giving mutual support and courage. Given that these four birds speak of the home, it might be that you are thinking of moving house, or expanding/improving your existing home. Work matters, too, are stable enough to be able to think about expansion in some way; you know that the hard work and achievements you've manifested have given you a solid grounding to proceed, perhaps in a new direction or Endeavour.

V
Five of Wands

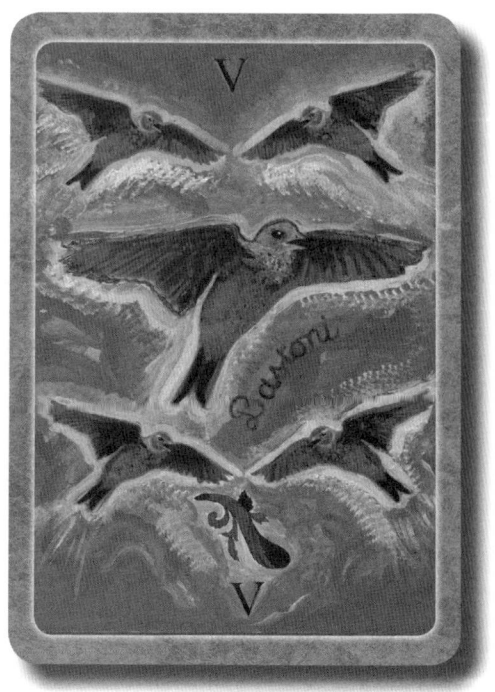

Drawn Reversed

Sometimes, the secure background of a secure home and family is not a part of our experience, so we have to create our own imprint of stability. This can be a life-long struggle and there are times when it seems insurmountable. It could also be that you have rejected your own background for some reason; whatever that reason, it's healthy to look objectively at your antecedents and try to understand, and have empathy with, your parents and ancestors. It's also the case that a particularly strong family can be stultifying as we find ourselves responsible for legacies we neither wanted nor asked for. But try to see beyond the immediate, and be grateful. It's only when you truly realize that your life is shaped primarily by your own attitude to things that you can fully integrate whatever is thrown at you.

Keywords

Testing; arguments and dispute, trying new ideas, conflict and power struggles. Possible illness.

Question Inspired by this Card:
How do I make something that seems to be bad into something that's good?

Drawn Upright

The five skylarks here are telling us that this is a time of conflict; but conflict can be a good thing, since all those involved are passionate enough about what they are doing to care deeply about it. However, it's important to resolve these conflicts creatively and to recognize that this current turbulence is all a counterpoint to the desired harmony; a see-saw of delicate balances that needs to come back to that central pivotal point. The tensions will result in an even better end result, and that's a good a place as any to start. Work backwards from what you wanted in the first place and you might be able to see objectively what the problem is. It could well be that the conflicts foretold by this card are the best route to a solution.

Drawn Reversed

Resolving conflicts is necessary, but sometimes the only recourse is to the law. You might be involved in legal disputes of some kind, and you'll need to tread carefully. Disputes, when not creatively settled, can lead to frustration and anger; and anger can lead to more dispute. If this vicious circle sounds familiar, then drawing this card reversed can be seen as an opportunity to see the problems for what they are, and not to get caught up in any more twisting and turning than is necessary. Sometimes, faced with an angry person, it's best to diffuse the situation rather than get drawn in. Silence can be a good friend.

VI
SIX OF WANDS

KEYWORDS
Triumph, and a good outcome. Struggles ended. Harmony after conflict, a resolution.

QUESTION INSPIRED BY THIS CARD:
WHAT IS MY TRUE REWARD?

DRAWN UPRIGHT

The skylarks here stand for spiritual illumination and practical inspiration, and now you're able to reap the results of your own ability to inspire others. Maybe your leadership qualities are recognized, and a promotion or award of some kind is coming your way. This sort of reward is related to the material world, but as with all matters related to the fiery Wands, the world of the spirit is equally important, especially in a card as balanced as the 6. It could be that you have achieved an inner strength and mastery born of a long-term practice or discipline; yoga, meditation or similar. If this doesn't fit, then perhaps you would benefit from such a practice in order to balance the material side of your life with the spiritual.

VII
Seven of Wands

Drawn Reversed

Feeling unappreciated; troubles caused by others; powerlessness; tedium.

It might be time to sit back and wait for a current dispute or argument to run its course, knowing that nothing you can do is going to help. This is a difficult realization to achieve if you have a natural inclination to "sort" things on behalf of others. In the meantime, look to your internal resources and see this as a way of learning to be patient, to plod on with what you're doing, in a quiet and unobtrusive way. Keep your head down to avoid any flying missiles, whether they be material or of the spirit. Above all, don't take any negative influences or adverse comments personally. Rise above it all, just like those skylarks, knowing that it will pass. Don't get personally involved!

Keywords

Courage; steadfastness, a lone struggle; self-belief.

Question Inspired by This Card:
How am I inspired by adversity?

Drawn Upright

Sometimes, when it seems as though the world is against us, we have to go right to the very depths of ourselves to find out exactly what it is that we do believe in. This can be a bit of a baptism of fire when we meet with opposition, but should be seen as a fantastic opportunity for finding our true purpose and seeing just how much inner strength we have. It might sounds like a hideous cliché, but difficult times really are character building; adversity gives us a chance to shine, to stretch ourselves, to become more alive and invigorated and resilient purely because of the struggle. The seven skylarks here tell us that this is the time that our mettle is being tested, and we'll be bigger, better, brighter than before, able to go on to do great things.

Drawn Reversed

Sometimes, conditions can seem to be so adverse, with maybe even friends becoming enemies, that our courage fails and all we want to do is run away and hide. You have to acknowledge that doing this might be okay for the time being, but that there will be a need at some point to come back and face your challenges. This is a great opportunity to turn your weaknesses into strengths; if you feel you are drowning, then learn to swim. It's tempting to want it all to go away and for things to be as they were before, but chances are that this former reality was a little stultifying and dull. Right now your confidence is at an all-time low; until it returns, be kind to yourself, make a list of all the good things in your life. And give yourself the sort of advice that you would give to a very good friend.

VIII
Eight of Wands

Keywords
New horizons; rapid movement; far-flung places; expansion.

Question inspired by this card:
What do I really want next?

Drawn Upright

Things are moving now so rapidly that it can be hard to take stock of exactly what's going on. These eight skylarks sweep you off your feet, whether it's in matters of the heart, work, new opportunities, or of having so many ideas that you almost can't decide which one to priorities so you end up trying to do them all. However, the advantage of having so many plates spinning means that you have to become ultra orderly and efficient, and even though you might not have realized just how streamlined you can be, this is a skill that comes naturally through necessity. Your energy is flowing well, obstacles non-existent, and all the new opportunities in your life seem to the

harmoniously linked. You are meeting all the new people you need to meet, and there's a great synchronicity in your life right now. Go for it!

DRAWN REVERSED

There may be delays, frustrations, misunderstandings, and problems in communications which can get so bad that relationships might be coming to an end, whether these are to do with work or love life. Nothing seems to be going according to plan, no matter how much hard work you're putting in. You feel like you're banging your head against a brick wall. However, in amidst all this angst and frustration, it's as well to hang on to the fact that in a few weeks' time, you'll know precisely that everything happened for the right reasons. Stop trying so hard, then you'll stop being frustrated. Stop trying to control things so much; surrender to the bigger picture in the absolute certainty that there *is* a bigger picture!

IX
NINE OF WANDS

KEYWORDS

A final hurdle to face; nearing the light at the end of the tunnel; the darkest hour before dawn.

QUESTION INSPIRED BY THIS CARD:
WHAT CAN REALLY HELP ME?

DRAWN UPRIGHT

You're nearly there, but not quite! Feeling battered by a struggle that you can now thankfully put behind you, nevertheless, in order to get to where you need to be, you still need to muster up all your internal powers and resources to make that one, final effort. And it's this effort which is proving difficult. The cliché "light at the end of the tunnel" and "the darkest hour is just before dawn" apply to these nine kingfishers. When we're in the midst of the struggle we don't have too much time to think, driven by essence and adrenalin. Once we don't need to be in crisis mode, it's almost as though there's a process of grieving, we miss that feeling of constantly being tense and on edge. But now is the time to allow yourself to relax, safe in the knowledge that the worst is over, and that easier, more creative and more fulfilling times are ahead.

DRAWN REVERSED

The sheer grind of recent events in your life may have made you run down and ill, unable to go on without help. But you are inclined to try to struggle on alone, trying to make everything fit and unwilling or unable to ask for help. You have to ask yourself why you want to carry this burden all alone. Imagine that a friend of yours was in the same situation; wouldn't you want to help? The success you have struggled for is within easy reach although you might have to prepare yourself for the fact that it might not happen quite as quickly as you want it to; all you need to do is make sure that you, yourself, are able to enjoy it when it comes.

X
Ten of Wands

Keywords
World-weariness; burdens; obligations; resignation.

Question inspired by this card:
How do integrate all my experiences?

Drawn Upright
You seem to have spent a lifetime working hard to realize your dreams, and everything you ever wanted, you have! However, there's vast difference between happiness and contentment, and you still feel almost an obligation to drive forward for more, as if the very struggle to succeed is an end in itself. It might not be time for you to retire yet, but all the same you perhaps need to gain perspective on things, to be able to stand and stare for a while rather than the constant pushing and pushing. You feel a colossal responsibility for all the successes in your life, and you feel that you have made yourself responsible for others, too, but this is a false supposition. You

XI
The Queen of Wands

are responsible only for yourself, and it might be time to start delegating some of the many tasks that lie between you and your being able to enjoy the fruits of your labors. In stepping back, we can find new inspiration.

Drawn Reversed

You may have many responsibilities, but you feel that the balance of your life is exactly right. You bear things well and have achieved a good understanding with people to whom you can delegate. You know how to enjoy time away from work, and whilst you're not the type to ever fully "switch off," you know the benefits of taking time out, that the world is a big place, and that a new horizon can help gain perspective and new inspiration. You are at a very good place in your life right now and there's no point in inventing things to worry about.

"Faith is the bird that feels the light when the dawn is still dark."
~Rabindranath Tagore

KEYWORDS
Friendly; infectious; acute; inventive.

DESCRIPTION
A beautiful young girl looks back at us, a friendly, quizzical look on her face. Her background is a fiery orange-red. In front of her are a family of cats; evidently a mother, a father, and three suckling kittens. This young queen wears a white dress and has long, tumbling brown hair.

DRAWN UPRIGHT
This young queen inspires everyone around her with an infectious enthusiasm; she is brimming over with ideas, and suggestions, and thoughts. Some of these will hit the mark, others will fall by the wayside, but it doesn't really matter; the essence of any idea will generally be "recycled" later, transformed into something else. It's easy for others to become caught up in the excitement, and they'll generally be happy to be involved, because the Queen of Wands is charming and dynamic and makes friends easily. She will also be delighted to introduce people to one another – a regular matchmaker, and this "type" is often to be found in some sort of Public Relations capacity. She has a temper, too, this Queen, and can get very upset about anything she feels, right or wrong, is injustice; but this fire fizzles out as quickly as it comes, and there's no need for anyone to take these flare-ups personally. The Queen of Wands likes a speedy pace of life and requires her companions and colleagues to be equally quick-witted and "ahead of the game."

DRAWN REVERSED
Obstacles; confusion; disruption; hyperactivity.

Energy, without focus or direction, can become like a whirlpool, sucking everything into its spiral but with no apparent constructive outcome. This is a good analogy for the reversed Queen of Wands. This card speaks of the sort of energy that can be manic, sweeping up everyone within reach, compelling them to become a part of the confusion. No matter how absurd or how extreme the level of confusion, it requires an iron will to resist such a magnetic draw. This confused energy can speak also of a maelstrom of emotional entanglements which you may find yourself caught up in; a necessary learning process, but one which you will nevertheless be glad to see the back of.

XII
THE KING OF WANDS

"Change will not come if we wait for some other person or some other time. We are the ones we've been waiting for. We are the change that we seek."

~Barack Obama

KEYWORDS
Optimism; keenness; choices.

DESCRIPTION
A young man, an idealistic and determined look on his face, looks to the skies, one hand raised up pointing towards the birds that fly about his head, a source of inspiration. This young King is elegantly dressed in a smart suit and tie, and his background is the red color that signifies the element of fire and all that it means; enthusiasm, passion, inspiration.

DRAWN UPRIGHT
Constantly stimulated, inspired, and excited by the many and varied possibilities that his wonderful life has to offer, the King of Wands is a young man who sometimes has *so* many choices that he either can't make up his mind which one to take, or ends up trying to do everything all at once! This is not an inability to make a firm decision; rather, he needs to see the necessity to surround himself with trusted advisers and friends to help him in these tricky decisions. This ability to see all sides of the situation and to look for the best in everything and everyone affects all aspects of his life; work, friendships, even relationships. The term "commitment phobic" springs to mind. However, the King of Wands is so charming and engaging that only those closest to him suffer from the exasperation and upset of his mercurial nature. This King loves to be taken away from the everyday and what he considers to be humdrum, and will drop everything to travel or seek new thrills. Although this is the card of a youthful male, the quality of youth need not be physical, but mental, and even internal. It's possible that in later years the King of Wands might look for someone that can be responsible for keeping him in check; a mother figure?

Drawn Reversed

Self-centered; caddish; heartless.

Reversed, the King of Wands can be the confidence trickster, the sharp-talking charmer who might take advantage of other peoples' good nature. In many ways this character is amoral and is unaware of the disruptive effect he can have on peoples' lives. He will stop at nothing to get what he wants, but then when he has the object of his desire, he is less interested in it and is eager to move onto the next thing. He is kept constantly on his toes pursuing and chasing. Reversed, the charm of the King of Wands can turn into something rather more predatory. He has no compunction about taking whatever hits his fancy, whether it's a heart or a bank balance, although in later years, life experience will teach him to have more respect for others.

God and Goddess of Wands

The final pair of cards in the suit of Wands is represented by the God and Goddess and a bird which belongs to myth and mystery. Here, we turn to India for our inspiration in the Gandaberunda, or Berunda, a fearsome bird that has its teeth in its beak and which often appears in Hindu temples, sometimes double-headed to reinforce its power.

XIII
The God of Wands

"I would rather learn from one bird how to sing than to teach 10,000 stars how not to dance."

~E.E. Cummings

Keywords
Focused, intelligent, intuitive, determined, kind.

Description
A beautiful Indian man is at one with the magnificent firebird that acts as his "vehicle," that is his familiar and the guise in which he appears to mortals. This God wears a crown to denote his royal status, and gazes ahead into the night sky, a determined, questing look on his face. The night sky behind him is studded with constellations, and he's surrounded by the flames of passion, inspiration and spiritual knowledge.

Drawn Upright
This is an inspirational man, who is able to bring out the best in others with no apparent effort, and in turn inspires deep affection, love, and loyalty

in those whose lives he touches. In many ways the perfect father, husband, or figure of authority, the God of Wands has a mischievous sense of fun running alongside his capable and responsible nature. One of the key facets of the King of Wands is his straightforward honesty, a trait he expects to see in other people. This man is the epitome of the ideal that we reap what we sow, and that we are able to create our own reality by means of the positive energies, wholehearted efforts and benevolent attitudes that we have are all able to choose.

Drawn Reversed

Self-doubt, questioning, restoration of faith.

Sometimes, no matter how hard we try to remain positive about the world in general, events collide to make us doubt for a short while our own optimism. Reversed, the God of Wands turns inward and seeks to question everything, a necessary process; but in so doing he must be careful not to let his own self-doubt taint the reality of the beautiful world that, deep down, he knows to be the true one.

XIV
The Goddess of Wands

"It's best to have failure happen early in life. It wakes up the Phoenix bird in you so you rise from the ashes."

~Anne Baxter

Keywords

Fieriness; dynamism; brilliance; flirtatiousness.

Description

A beautiful Asian woman looks tenderly down at the firebird that is her vehicle; i.e., the creature to whom this Goddess appears to mortals. She and the bird are one, but her soft beauty belies the apparent fearsomeness of the creature she hugs. The night sky, studded with constellations, forms a backdrop as she flies through it with fiery wings. To show her status as a divinity, the Goddess of Wands wears a crown and also has a golden halo. She wears rings on her index finger (indicative of mastery) and on the fourth finger, and a matching golden bangle. On her forehead is a six-pointed star.

Drawn Upright

A sparkling, vibrant bird, the skylark is a very appropriate bird for this rather flighty woman, although here, the Goddess is accompanied by her own firebird. This Goddess can be something of a conundrum in many ways. Although she is gregarious and likes to have people around her, she equally loves her own company and is the sort of person who will throw huge parties then drift away to do her own thing. Driven and dynamic, the Goddess of Wands is brimming over with ideas and has an oblique take on many aspects of life. If you need inventive and innovative notions about anything at all, this is the woman you need to call upon; but don't take her for granted, otherwise she'll become discouraged, for all her generosity; remember that she is of the element of fire and needs to be reassured, appreciated and acknowledged for her input and her generosity. The Goddess of Wands has an uncanny knack of generally getting her own way, but at the same time making everyone else feel good about the decision that was made. Possibly one of the best allies to have on your side, the Goddess very rarely gives up on people; however, once someone has stepped over the line, she will turn her back on them swiftly and cease all communication. The Goddess is a fine and loyal friend, and has no enemies at all – simply because she refuses to acknowledge their existence.

Drawn Reversed

Controlling; manipulative; jealous.

Here, this Goddess can be so eager to be appreciated that she can subsume herself in others' needs and then wonder why she is unhappy. The strong interest that she has in people, when reversed, can turn to resentment and impatience with them, and this can lead to anger and conflict. She will hold a grudge long after anyone else can remember what it was all about in the first place – including herself! Her need for attention can make her something of a drama queen and she can be apt to cause trouble simply to feed this need. Those caught up in her drama often stand back, reeling, wondering what just hit them, and consequently some people tend to be wary around her; once bitten, twice shy. Much of the cause of this conflict and the temper tantrums – and the sheer drama queen behavior – is because the reversed Goddess has not defined her purpose in life. She may need help to do this, because it's likely she can't see the wood for the trees!

THE SUIT OF SWORDS

Spade

The Element of Air Represented by the Seagull

The suit of swords is all about the intellect, the mind, logical analysis. The sword as a symbol of justice is an appropriate reminder of the meaning of these fourteen cards and, of course, the nature of the element itself. The Italian word for swords, Spade, is of course the name given to the suit in "normal" playing cards.

For the purposes of this tarot deck, we've chosen the seagull.

Like air people, the seagull is infinitely adaptable, and able to see the bigger picture, has a wide range of experiences because of the breadth of its travel. Soaring high above the

I
Ace of Swords

sea, carried by currents of sharp winds, the wings of the seagull glitter like swords against the bright sky.

Seagull people are liable to be analytical, clear thinking, and decisive. They don't suffer fools gladly and strive for truth and justice. Lateral thinkers, they are able to see all sides of an argument before making a decision. With a "seagull" person, you should un-expect the expected; there's a streak of eccentricity running through their veins. Where a flock of seagulls appears in a spread, be aware that thought and intellect takes priority over the feelings and emotions. Intuition is left on the back burner in favor of clear, sharp common sense.

Keywords
Transformation, innovation, focus, rapid change.

Question Inspired by this Card:
What Makes Me Think?

Drawn Upright

This lone seagull soars high into the air, cutting a swathe in the sky, direct, focused, sure. The sword, of course, is a symbol of justice but here it stands for the specific justice of karma, the law of cause and effect; what we reap, we sow. This might be a time of "instant karma," all about reconciling the past with current events and on into the future. Your intellect is sharpened and awareness heightened; this is a good time for any kind of work involving the mind. The sword signifies a clean sweep, too; a slicing-away of the past, clearing away dead wood to provide light and space for new growth. This is a good time for any new intellectual Endeavour.

Drawn Reversed

Much of life is about integration and harmony between all the opposing forces we're made of; the male/female polarity, the light and dark, the elements. The reversed ace of swords tells us that this balance is out of kilter and the intellect and the emotions are not working in that harmonic ideal. Consequently, the clarity of thought that's a keen part of the sword symbolism is skewed. It's possible that the success has bred arrogance and that it's time for a transformative change to redress this disharmony.

II
Two of Swords

Keywords
An uneasy peace; matched adversaries; the calm before the storm; opposition.

Question inspired by this card:
How do I encompass other peoples' needs without compromise?

Drawn Upright

This is the card of the stalemate. Adversaries, well-matched, who have reached a pause-point in their fighting, are each waiting for the other to make the next move. This doesn't necessarily mean human adversaries; rather, you might be feeling as though you are on the horns of a dilemma, trying to work out what's best to do next. At such times it's easy to put things off, or try to hope that the problem will go away. However, whilst this might sometimes be the best course of action, the two seagulls shown tell you that you're going to have to tackle a particular situation, if not head-on, then certainly after a period of observation from the sidelines. If there

III
Three of Swords

can be such a thing as "calm tension" then this is what you're experiencing. There's no need to keep looking over your shoulder, but you do need to be aware that you will soon have to play a next move and that this game is still very much in action.

Drawn Reversed

Conflict is a part of life, and despite our best efforts, sometimes we find ourselves involved in something we might have been doing our best to avoid. We are dragged into disputes for all sorts of reasons, some seemingly beyond our remit. But however these disputes have arisen, facing them courageously will only serve to make us stronger and less fearful. Whatever lies may be flying around, face them with integrity and rest easy in the knowledge that the truth will come out – although this doesn't always happen immediately. Have faith that there's a reason for the situation you find yourself in, and that the bigger picture will be revealed. Do not give in to your intellectual desire to try to steer events that are beyond your control.

KEYWORDS

Grief and heartache; an uneasy triangle; a great lesson.

QUESTION INSPIRED BY THIS CARD:
HOW DO I LEARN TO SEE THINGS DIFFERENTLY?

DRAWN UPRIGHT

This is a difficult card. It tells of a time of suffering and emotional trauma, possibly to do with a third party in a relationship, and the ensuing separation or conflict between the founder members of that relationship. Whilst sorrow and suffering are terrible to endure, they do give us a greater depth and understanding and ultimately help us to empathize with others in the same situation. And it really is true that time is a great healer. Nevertheless, it's natural to feel grief for any sort of loss, and this card does bring change with it, a change which initially won't be very welcome. You may experience a period of shock, too, as you readjust. That said, events in your life always happen when we are strong enough, and ready for them. You'll soon find that you emerge, new and shiny and happy, from this chrysalis of sorrow.

DRAWN REVERSED

It's time to let go of past hurts, since life, after all, is short. This isn't a process that can be rushed because we do need time to assimilate, but as with any period of mourning or grief, there comes a time when you wake up and feel different; you have recovered. If you're not quite at this point just yet, you soon will be, and you'll be ready to move on and restore all the things in your life that you had thought were missing. And everything will be even better than before because of this watershed period in your life. You will realize the value of the lessons you've learned.

IV
The Four of Swords

Keywords
A pause; withdrawing; quiet contemplation.

Question inspired by this card:
How do I find peace of mind?

Drawn Upright

After conflict, illness, stressful times or the like, we need to take time out to recuperate and gather our resources, to replenish our strength and process everything that's happened. Effectively, this could amount to a holiday, but not necessarily in the traditional sense of the word. Here, the four seagulls speak of the need for a retreat, a contemplative time, a period of meditation. It always seems to be an odd thing that we ensure that our cars are serviced regularly and yet we often neglect our physical and mental health until we're almost at breaking point. It's time for some tender loving care for your mind, body and spirit – and no-one is going to be able to do this for you, you have to do it for yourself. Such a break will mean that you emerge re-energized, equipped and ready for whatever is next, having clarified your mind and replenished your soul.

DRAWN REVERSED

Drawn reversed, the four seagulls tell you that it's time to come out into the world again, to actively seek company and a decent social life. You might have experienced personal losses of one sort or another, but it's now time to put all this behind you and look to a fully-integrated future. Part of this process might involve a physical clearing-out of things you don't need any more, as well as a mental process of defining what you want, where your boundaries are, and what goals you want to achieve.

V
FIVE OF SWORDS

Keywords
A difficult lesson; plans rethought, situations changed.

Question Inspired by this Card:
How do I know when it's time to change tactics?

Drawn Upright

Sometimes, you can fight and fight and fight and yet things still don't go your way; in fact, the tide of events is completely contrary to what you've been fighting for, and you might be feeling a sense of failure or loss and just want to "give up," tired of struggling. The old saying "sticks and stones may break my bones but words can never hurt me" is in fact not true; words can leave a resonance of pain that outlasts any physical bruising, and in drawing this card the five seagulls here might be telling you that harsh or untrue words have been aimed at you, and they're wearing you down. Or these words might be being spoken behind your back, and there's nothing you can do about such underhand tactics. Sometimes when we try to protest about such matters, we feed the flames rather than damping them. There's a lot of pride involved, too, in wanting to set matters straight, but in this case it might be better to let sleeping dogs lie and simply behave in an elegant and dignified manner, hard though this might be to countenance.

Drawn Reversed

It takes a great deal of courage to accept defeat, but there's a strangely satisfying cathartic process that happens when we do so. The "defeat" suddenly dissolves, as though everything we were fighting for never really existed. This is a very liberating feeling, and it could be time for you to experience it for yourself. What will come in its place is a feeling of clarity, freedom, and an invigorating sense of leaving the past behind and striding forward to healthy new pastures. Cutting your losses isn't just a material process, but an emotional one too, allowing you to sever ties with hindrances that have been sapping your energy.

VI
Six of Swords

Keywords
Healing energies; reconciliation; a journey, conscious decisions.

Question inspired by this card:
How do I learn to believe that things are better?

Drawn Upright

As with all the "6" numbered cards, these seagulls speak of harmony and reconciliation. For now, the swords of conflict are put away and we can look forward to a calmer future after much travail. Your problems are moving away, easily, as you've managed to detach from them. This conscious detachment has a fundamental part to play in that release. From now on, everything will improve; love life, finances, career matters. Most importantly, you have a deeper understanding of the true meaning of the phrase "a conscious decision." The sword stands for intellectual clarity, the sharp mind that can cut through nonsense to get to the heart of the matter. Here, you have managed to apply that process to your own self and you have a new, profound level of your own sense of self that's part of an emerging, coherent bigger picture.

DRAWN REVERSED

You feel as though you're right in the eye of the storm, clinging onto the edge of a tornado in the calm spot, whilst knowing that the tornado isn't yet over. Enjoy this calm as much as you can; take a short break if possible to gird your loins for what's to come. Grit and tenacity are required, for sure. You'll find that the storm you're expecting won't be half as bad as you thought, and much of this will be down to the state of mind you're in, and in the aspects of your life that you know you can prepare against the worst possibility. Above all, see what happens if you stop trying to "solve" the problem. Take courage from this card; the agony will be over soon and the storm clouds will clear to reveal a brilliantly clear sky!

VII
SEVEN OF SWORDS

KEYWORDS
Scattershot efforts; trying to do too much; skimming the surface of things.

QUESTION INSPIRED BY THIS CARD:
WHERE ARE MY EFFORTS BEST PLACED?

DRAWN UPRIGHT

The seven seagulls here bring with them a sort of seething, boiling energy, riven with innovatory ideas and new thoughts that speed through the mind at a rate of knots. The need to get these ideas out means that you're working on lots of different things at the same time, all of which are feeding each other. This is all incredibly exciting and stimulating but even in the midst of all this you're aware of the need to rein in, intellectually, to keep hold of mental discipline, and that some of the many projects you're leaning towards do need a level of research and diligent application. Such sensible concerns might make you feel like you're being "slowed down;" however, these concerns are for your ultimate long term benefit. The research indicated by this card can also signify plotting and planning; don't be tempted to "end game" or try to machinate an outcome. Enjoy being in the moment.

DRAWN REVERSED

Sometimes, when we are besieged with ideas, it's so difficult to decide which one to get on with that we end up doing either all of them very badly, or none of them at all as we ditch project after project in despair. This card warns of the need to provide a proper structure to what you're doing, and that if you decide to involve others, of the need to protect your copyright. Time spent on such matters will serve you well in the long run and will actually have the effect of liberating your mind against the possibility of there being deceptive people around you. Deceptions may not be just about intellectual matters, but could concern practical issues; there might be a troublemaker in your midst who will twist the truth to their own advantage, a "crazy maker." Be on your guard.

VIII
Eight of Swords

Keywords
Complex problems; lack of perspective; milling thoughts.

Question inspired by this card:
What's the real issue that's concerning me?

Drawn Upright

Sometimes, you just can't see the wood for the trees, and a certain situation has you going round in circles as a result. The eight seagulls depicted on this card, and the eight swords that combine to make a cage, describe just such a situation. You might even be having sleepless nights as a result, as your thoughts churn around endlessly seeking a solution that seems to be ever more elusive as you're becoming worn down and tired. What you need now is some perspective; it could well be that someone close is trying to tell you this but that you're so embroiled in the particular problems that are facing you, that you can't even hear what they are saying! So in fact,

IX
Nine of Swords

drawing this card, and the message that it bears, is a fortunate sign that things are about to turn around for you – if you follow the advice that it's giving.

Drawn Reversed

You're experiencing a feeling of renewed hope, release, excitement at all the possibilities that are now laid before you after a time of great difficulties. It's as though you've not only seen the light at the end of the tunnel, but you're standing in it, the full brilliance of the sunlight hitting you in a wave of optimism and inspiration. Be aware that you don't need to try too hard or try to do too much too soon; take baby steps into this startling new light, and don't try to run before you can walk. There are good times ahead which you thoroughly deserve after everything that's happened to you!

KEYWORDS
Stress; insoluble problems; anxiety.

QUESTION INSPIRED BY THIS CARD:
DO I REALLY NEED TO WORRY ABOUT ANYTHING?

DRAWN UPRIGHT

So, you have worries? It's possible that you're trying to pretend that they don't exist, that you're trying to sweep them under the carpet. But you know that the lump in the middle of the floor is there for a reason! Whatever those anxieties are, it's important that you tackle them head on, in the cold light of day, just so that you know exactly where you are. They could be worse than you think, but it's generally the case that, under really close scrutiny, they're actually *not* as bad as you had anticipated, and it's likely that this is the case here, too. You can also ask other people to help; this might be expert advice in, say, financial matters, or the practical sort of help that you would be glad to give to a close friend of yours – so do ask for it yourself. It's also the case that we are quick to help others, but find it hard to ask for help ourselves, and if there's a possibility that this is the case, then you need to ask yourself why. Giving has to be on equal terms, after all.

DRAWN REVERSED

You've come through a difficult time, but the worst is definitely over, and now you need to knuckle down and get to work to make up for lost ground. This might be a bit of an uphill struggle at first but you'll find help in unexpected quarters if you remain open to all possibilities. Keep an open mind to new and innovative ideas which might involve ways for you to forge ahead. The challenges you face are far from insurmountable and you feel pleasantly excited at the thought of turning things around – a possibility of which you are now certain.

X
Ten of Swords

Keywords
Betrayal of trust; confidences placed with the wrong person; disappointment.

Question inspired by this card:
What are the really good things in my life?

Drawn Upright

It's always good to trust someone implicitly, and share everything with them. But beware the person who doesn't share back with you equally. In drawing this card, it's possible that you have placed trust in someone who is unworthy of it, and they have betrayed that trust. This might seem to you that they have no respect in you – but ultimately the truth is that this person has no self-respect. This will always be a problem for them, but for you this need be a problem no longer. This betrayal may have happened by the spoken or possibly the written word. It's likely that because of it a certain chapter in your life is coming to a close; a relationship, a friendship, a job, even the place that you live. All are up for scrutiny. Most importantly, remember that although you might feel that you have been naive, the innocence of a child is also something that we should all aspire to, and just because one person has been unworthy of you doesn't mean to say that the world is made of such people. Hold your head up, knowing that you have done nothing wrong, and that the circumstances that have arisen will only be good for you in the long run.

DRAWN REVERSED

Sometimes, when we expect the worst thing to happen, then it does, almost by default. Now, with another mindset we can see that the "worst" thing is never as bad as we think it is, and by changing our attitudes and beliefs, then we can effectively change the world. It's time to apply some of this positive-thinking stratagem to your own life, and to know that so long as we are alive and on the planet that anything is possible! The only thing that would stand in the way of this is if you have a deep-rooted depression; sometimes when this is the case, it's hard to realize it. However, in drawing this card you might want to investigate the possibility that the first step towards fixing such a condition is to admit to the possibility, because then you put yourself on a position to be able to do something about it.

XI
QUEEN OF SWORDS

Minor Arcana

"I don't ask for the meaning of the song of a bird or the rising of the sun on a misty morning. There they are, and they are beautiful."

~Pete Hamill

KEYWORDS

Inquisitive; insightful; acute powers of observation; objective.

DESCRIPTION

A lone seagull flies above the head of its Queen, who reclines, relaxed and beautiful, a come-hither look on her face. Mischievous and flirty, nevertheless the sword which is the symbol of this suit rests by a plate; on the plate some pieces of fruit cheekily make a face as though to temper the sharpness of the steel. Further sharp barbs appear in the thorns of the rose that the Queen holds; the red rose is also, of course, a symbol of love. A beautiful white cat curls, drowsy but not asleep, on her lap, and a crescent moon appears in the silver sky.

DRAWN UPRIGHT

Although this card belongs to a Queen, as with all Tarot cards of a distinct sex, remember that it's the qualities of the figure we're seeking to understand, which reach beyond the vagaries of mere gender. Here, we find someone who is logical, insightful, perceptive, and with all the detachment associated with such powers of objectivity. There's not much that gets past this person, and on occasion they are detached enough to leave room to maneuver in even their surest instincts; in other words, this person takes nothing for granted. This mindset means that the Queen of Swords is hardly ever surprised, and could be seen by some to be cynical – but she really isn't. Combine this with the ability to grasp any situation quickly and accurately, and with a self-possession rarely seen, and you find someone that can be quick to turn any situation to their advantage.

The Queen of Swords has great oracular powers, too, and can talk round any situation with a skilful use of words. In some circumstances this is the card of the diplomat, the spin doctor or the politician. However, a finely-attuned instinct for a person or a situation doesn't necessarily mean that there's an ability to see much beyond the immediate moment, and sometimes this Queen is hampered by a lack of organizational skills. Once she gets to realize this, however, she will objectively see the weakness and will make sure that she has effective help in this area.

The detached quality, too, can be off putting, and some might see her as being aloof. This means that she might find it difficult to find an equal partner in her love-life, although it's not usually a problem in business. What does it take to crack that reserve? Ruled by the head, as with all the suit of swords, and with a keen love of language, this Queen will react well to word-play, puns – and love letters, particularly if written by hand, which she will secretly read over and over.

DRAWN REVERSED

Disengaged; lonely; resentful; lack of empathy, lack of humor.

All the intriguing qualities which make the Queen of Swords such an interesting character can, when reversed, make her very difficult to understand and to deal with. Although she is the ultimate observer of others, she also has a keen ability to observe herself, too, and this, ability for self-observation, combined with a keen critical faculty, can make her own sternest critic. She will strive for perfection for its own sake, and will often work long hours, neglecting her social life and running the risk of offending her friends – so her isolation could become even more pronounced. The rose that the Queen holds is beautiful, but the barbs can be sharp; sometimes the barbs of her critical tongue can offend, since the Queen of Swords doesn't always realize the effect that words can have on people, and she might sometimes be accused of being heartless and cruel. If you have drawn this card and any of this description fits, remember to be kind to yourself. Take time occasionally to do nothing but stand and stare. Try to re-engage with your emotions and to put yourself in others' shoes by imagining how they might feel in certain circumstances. Enjoy your life and the planet around you, your friends and family. Above all, the Queen of Swords should apply that useful objectivity to herself, and see herself as others might see her. She should remember not to take herself too seriously, and to laugh occasionally!

XII
KING OF SWORDS

"Hold fast to your dreams, for without them life is a broken winged bird that cannot fly."

~Langston Hughes

KEYWORDS
Charismatic, intelligent, spontaneous.

DESCRIPTION
The Sun, symbolic of the male element, hangs golden-red in the silver sky, above the head of the handsome King of Swords. This man looks authoritarian, but not overly so, and he holds the sword, symbol here of the intellect and the element of air, almost casually, displaying it rather than intending to use it as a weapon. Three seagulls hover around him. He's dressed elegantly, and has a keen, satisfied expression on his face. This King is confident and well-pleased with himself.

DRAWN UPRIGHT
Remember that although a card may carry a male figure, it's the qualities of the card that

matter. Look beyond sex to gain a sense of the person we're talking about.

The King of swords is charming and seductive, quick-witted and intelligent. He sounds like the perfect man; however, a youthful egotism sometimes blurs the picture. He's the sort of man who will always put his own needs first, although he's clever to disguise this where necessary. This does mean, though, that he can inadvertently cause hurt to anyone who might be in the way of his driven forward motion. But don't mistake this man for a fop. His youthful "devil may care" attitude mean that he's prone to talking huge risks, stepping where angels fear to tread, and rushing headlong into some idea or scheme, looking only ahead. If the scheme works out he's delighted, and even if things "fail" he's liable to hide any disappointment and show a confident face, putting it down to experience before rapidly forgetting all about it. You'll never find this King contemplating his navel. He's just not that type, and pours scorn on any signs of flimsy new-age spirituality, meditation, self-analysis. That said, he's secretly aware of the fact that there's "something else" which he currently lacks the maturity to investigate further. For now, though, he's happy to be his own impetuous, sometimes-rakish self. Good company because of his dry wit and hysterically-sharp observations, the King of Swords is unlikely to come to your aid in a time of real need, so any friendship should be taken as what it is; of surface value only.

DRAWN REVERSED

Egotistical and self-centered; immoral; one-dimensional.

A lack of empathy and no interest in the needs of others can make a reversed King of Swords a difficult character to understand, especially since he will often operate completely outside the parameters of what's acceptable in terms of ethical or moral behavior. Sometimes it can take a while to realize that this is what's happening. In business deals with this type of character, you need to watch your back. The tricky thing is that this King won't even realize that he's doing anything wrong, since catering to his own needs and desires above all else is an endemic part of his personality. The long and short is that even when drawn upright, the King of

Swords can be untrustworthy; reversed, there's no doubt that this is the case. Because his "rules" are different, anyone else simply can't play the same game – and he's unable to compromise simply because he's unable to understand. Dealings with such a person are unlikely to be repeated except by someone who believes that they might be able to "change" the nature of the King of Swords, and wants to prove this point by showing a good example. This is, unfortunately, unlikely to work.

God and Goddess of Swords

The final pair in the deck of Swords is the God and Goddess. Here, they are accompanied by a mythical bird that represents the Condor, one of the most sacred creatures in the Latin American bird myths. The Condor is famed for its far-reaching overview; it is able to fly for ten miles without once flapping its wings, able to simply soar on the air, effortlessly.

XIII
God of Swords

> *"Perfect as the wing of a bird may be, it will never enable the bird to fly if unsupported by the air. Facts are the air of science. Without them a man of science can never rise."*
>
> ~Ivan Pavlov

KEYWORDS
Intellectually powerful; opinionated; forceful.

DESCRIPTION
Against a spangly silvery background, the God of Swords gazes determinedly locked in a mutual embrace with his bird, the seagull. He wears an elaborate headdress and similarly ornate jeweler, as befits his status. His mouth is open as though he's expressing an opinion.

DRAWN UPRIGHT
The God of Swords can be a challenging character to live with. No matter what his role in life, he is always quick to voice his opinion, sometimes in voluble exchanges, maybe in writing, since he is very able at expressing these opinions in any medium, but is perhaps at his most persuasive as an orator. And he feels the need to express these opinions whether or not he is invited to do so, a trait which can sometimes cause irritation in others – especially members of his family!

Having said that, if the God of Swords is on your side, you will find no more effective advocate, since his arguments are extremely shrewd; if you have him as an enemy, however, beware, because his cutting arguments are sometimes used effectively to divide and rule, and he can be an extremely persuasive person. He is interested in the finer and trickier points of any intellectual discipline – for example, the law. Able to move happily in any society, the God of Swords will find people in all walks of life that share his interests. Ultimately, this God would like to change the world in some way, and may indeed succeed in this aim.

In relationships, the God of Swords needs someone who likes to play devil's advocate, since nothing stimulates him so much as an intellectual challenge or argument. This God cannot stand emotional neediness in anyone, and will cut and run at the first sign of it.

Drawn Reversed

Argumentative; cruel; moody.

His argumentative nature means that the God of Swords will sometimes pick a fight just for the sake of it, especially if he's allowed himself to become bored or disinterested in something. Also, his demeanor is naturally aggressive, so often people of lesser intelligence will see this as offensive, and this could lead to trouble; there's a bloody-minded side to the God of Swords that will enjoy this sort of conflict. As a result, it's easy for people to be alienated by this character, and as a result, he can become isolated – which makes him naturally more predisposed to anger, a vicious circle.

A natural propensity for anger can make the God of Swords a tricky person to have to deal with, and when this anger turns to cruelty, the object of his derision can end up feeling battered and torn. A natural inclination to mistrust people means that the God of Swords can sometimes be a very dark and moody character indeed. Dramatic flashes of temper, and an almost bipolar series of unexpected reactions means that anyone dealing with him will have to have a great deal of understanding and patience.

VIV
Goddess of Swords

"A fish may love a bird, but where would they live?"

~Drew Barrymore

KEYWORDS
Independent; cool; witty and intelligent; forthright and loyal.

DESCRIPTION
Against a tumult of silver and glitter the Goddess of Swords looks back at us. Her bird rests its head under her arm, wings unfurled. The Goddess wears heavily ornamental jewelry including a spangled headband; she also has feathers in her hair.

DRAWN UPRIGHT
As befits a Goddess, this is a very powerful woman. Her incisive mind to means that she's likely to be in a position of some authority, and she is able to cut to the chase and see the bigger picture; she has an eagle-eyed way of analysis. She may well have a companion, but despite this she carries with her an air of independence; she speaks of "I" rather than "we" as a matter of course. Any long-term partner for such a woman will need to understand this implicitly and might cultivate a similar air of independence. She cannot stand to be tied down or bound in any way; for this Goddess, freedom is paramount and she finds any kind of constriction absolutely horrifying. If there is any display of neediness in anyone she has to deal with, then she's likely to cut off from them completely. It's likely that this Goddess will have many relationships, some of which may be seen to be quite unconventional by the outside world. In fact, her entire way of life may be viewed as strange or incomprehensible to outsiders; however, the Goddess of Swords is good at keeping many aspects of her life away from the scrutiny of small-minded people. A tough cookie, this Goddess; she has a scientific way of thinking and a forensic line of questioning things.

The Goddess of Swords has had, and continues to have, an adventurous life which encompasses a wide range of different experiences; she is quite fearless, and all these experiences have added to her knowledge of the world, understanding of the people in it, and, ultimately, her wisdom. She will find a level of happiness and contentment in the smallest of things, but always has an underlying feeling of restlessness, which is a great "driver."

Drawn Reversed

Cold; heartless; spiteful; disengaged from people.

The Goddess of Swords is very much engaged in her own thought processes, can be very "heady." This, combined with her fierce independence and lack of a need for anyone else, can mean that she can become inadvertently alienated from any people who, viewing her from the outside, find that she is quite a fearsome person to have to deal with; she can appear to be unapproachable and strict. Her critical faculty is such that she may pick fault with things unnecessarily, and might seem to be dissatisfied with the sorts of things that others would take for granted as part of life's little foibles; again, another factor which is unlikely to make her very popular. The Goddess of Swords can also be stubborn to the point of not doing herself any favors, intent on the empirical value of the "rules" rather than the spirit in which they were made.

THE SUIT OF COINS

Denari

The Element of Earth Represented by the Wren

The suit of coins is, as you might imagine, all about the material world, in all its aspects. The cards here represent physical wealth (and also the lack of it), abundance, buildings, possessions, riches. The farthing, an old British coin that is now obsolete, featured a wren since, like the bird, the coin was small currency.

For the purposes of this deck we've chosen the wren. Often in the material world we need to remember that less is more; there's an old Scottish saying "mony a mickle maks a muckle," which means that lots of little things add up to a lot, and there's a wonderful tale about the wren that reflects this idea. The Eagle, sovereign of the entire bird kingdom, decided one day that he'd challenge all the birds to a race to see who could fly the highest. The eagle, believing the wren to be too small and insignificant to even be a contender, doesn't even invite him to take part.

Accordingly, all the birds set off and one by one drop away, leaving the eagle well ahead. As he reached the highest point possible, the eagle shouts out his victory; but the moment he turns to begin his descent, the wren, who has secreted himself in the thick feathers around the back of the eagle's neck, pops out and flies just that little bit higher. The other birds all witness this, and on his return to earth, the eagle is suitably chastened at having overlooked the fact that he's been beaten by a bird so small.

Cards belonging to this suit relate to people who are very much "earthed" in the real world, practical and reliable, trustworthy, hard working, and generally with solid values. Earth people aspire to amass wealth in many different ways and in many different forms. They are liable to consider the value not only of any potential purposes, but will weigh up the pros and cons of any decisions that need to be made, too. What's on the table, here and now, is going to be more important than intuition or instinct.

The final four cards of this suit see our birds shapeshifting into the form of humans and Gods, and with the deities, the idea of coins flips to its alternative name, Pentacles, and we delve deep into the magic of the Owl, in honor of the tale from the Mabinogion of Blodeudd, the beautiful woman made of flowers, who was turned into an owl.

I
Ace of Coins

Keywords
A windfall; financial gain; material benefits.

Question inspired by this card:
What does wealth mean to me?

Drawn Upright

The ace is of course the "seed" card, and the lone wren here tells us that this is the beginning of a fortunate time, financially. It might be that a new scheme will be more successful than you'd anticipated, or that there might be an unexpected windfall; a prize or an inheritance, for example. Although this suit does govern wealth and abundance, this doesn't always mean direct financial gain. You may have made significant efforts with something and the rewards come to you as an increase in salary or a bonus of some kind. It's a wonderful thing to be able to point to the direct financial benefits associated with hard work and talent, but there's also an element of luck that comes with the Ace of Coins; it seems that fortune is smiling on you now and it's a good time to put plans into action, knowing that the odds are stacked cosmically in your favor.

Drawn Reversed

Money is only useful in what it can purchase, whether that be material goods, an experience, or perhaps best of all, freedom. It's important to see it for what it is – a means to an end, rather than the end of the journey in itself. Yes, it's good to save, but be careful that this prudent stash of cash doesn't turn into a miserly hoard. We only realize what we've got when we're able to give some of it away, and in giving freely, wholeheartedly, and unconditionally we become empowered. True wealth doesn't lie in hard currency, but in the inner depths of the soul and concerns with issues that go beyond the material. You need to strike a balance in order to understand the true meaning of abundance. In drawing this card, too, there could be money worries, concerns about making ends meet. You might need to put some of your passions to one side for the time being as you go through a period of retrenchment, with an eye to the bigger picture and the awareness that money can't buy happiness.

II
Two of Coins

Minor Arcana   179

KEYWORDS
Balance, both financial and ethical; interesting opportunities, hard work.

QUESTION INSPIRED BY THIS CARD:
WHAT DOES WEALTH MEAN TO OTHERS?

DRAWN UPRIGHT

The two wrens depicted here tell of new skills, new opportunities, and a partnership that could lead to satisfaction in general and financial success in particular. This will probably mean a period of quite intense work during which the work/home life balance might become unsettled; be aware of this and try not to take absolutely everything quite so seriously. It's important to enjoy what you're doing and to have some fun with it. The thought of having an ally, in whatever part of your life, is a wonderful thing; someone to take up the slack from time to time and lend an ear and a new perspective is valuable indeed. And this card says that you have that ally, someone who is totally on your side. This is likely to do with work, but you may also find that a different kind of partner will lend support exactly where it's needed, allowing you the freedom to do what you need to do.

DRAWN REVERSED

When drawn reversed, the two of coins brings a message of financial instability, misplaced trust, and irresponsibility in terms of material assets. That's not to say that you need to make paranoid efforts to protect what you have, but that you do need to take a good clear look at your assets and liabilities, rather than avoiding the truth which is something that you might have previously been inclined to do. Only in this way can you restore the imbalances that might have occurred. It's easy to blame external factors for a financial mess, but in this case you do need to look to yourself for the truth although another party may be able to help with a solution. It's important that you examine everything thoroughly in order to avoid possible trouble, either in the sense of loss of goodwill or the productive energy of others.

III
Three of Coins

Keywords
Hard work rewarded; a team effort; skill and mastery attained.

Question inspired by this card:
What is my reward?

Drawn Upright

An auspicious card indeed, the three wrens here indicate that you are gaining rewards and recognition for your efforts. These efforts may have required many years learning and honing a craft, and you have diligently applied these skills to the work which is now at last so highly valued. It's quite right that you should be proud of your achievement at the same time as recognizing the important part that has been played by others; you value the true worth of collaboration where it's needed. You are at the height of your profession, and you've got the respect that you deserve.

You may also be contemplating learning an entirely new set of skills, perhaps branching out into something you've always been passionate

IV
FOUR OF COINS

about but have been cautious about developing. Maybe you just haven't had the time, or maybe you lacked confidence. You may be taking a leap in the dark, but you know that now is the time to go for it!

DRAWN REVERSED

Sometimes, we have to put in a lot of time and unseen hard work into making something a success, and you may have stinted in this. It's possible that you've tried to take shortcuts and you're now paying the price. A lack of commitment and focus could be the cause – or sheer laziness. It could also be that you made the wrong choice in something and that you're finding it hard to dredge up any enthusiasm. If this is the case then it might be time to cut your losses, take this whole experience as a lesson learned, and seek pastures new. Making a fresh start can be challenging and difficult, but it also opens up some exciting possibilities if you dare to use your imagination!

KEYWORDS
Stability; responsibility; security

QUESTION INSPIRED BY THIS CARD:
WHAT IS THE TRUE MEANING OF SECURITY?

DRAWN UPRIGHT
The number four is the number of stability; think of the four legs of a table, or the four walls of a house. And given that the suit of coins signifies riches in whatever form they may take but with an emphasis on the financial aspect, then it's easy to see what these four wrens are telling us. This is a time of financial stability, prudence, the rewards of diligent effort. The power of wealth provides a solid foundation upon which to build, but beware of a tendency towards dullness, which can be the result when the making of money can be a means in itself rather than the means to an end. Financial security is one thing, but personal security – born of a strong family background and feeling good about yourself – are not constructed from money. Now that you have such financial security, you might be asking yourself, what next? The temptation is to build on it, but occasionally it's also nice to take some risks; otherwise you could become stodgily dedicated to the gathering of more and more wealth rather than allowing yourself to enjoy the pleasure that it can bring you.

DRAWN REVERSED
Security isn't just about finances. The poorest people on the planet can have a different kind of security, the spiritual kind, which comes from close family attachments, love, and a feeling of community. It could be that you are facing some of your innermost fears, coming up to a watershed in your life, in which you question the meaning of many of the things you are doing. Sometimes it's hard to admit our deepest feelings and deep-rooted fears to other people, but in doing so we can also liberate ourselves, realizing that the need to gather material riches might be covering up uncertainty in other areas. By opening yourself up to such a possibility, you'll experience a new period of personal growth and fulfillment.

V
Five of Coins

Keywords
Loss; despair; a struggle; pessimism

Question inspired by this card:
How do I find the good in every situation?

Drawn Upright

On the face of things, the five wrens here don't carry a particularly happy message. They foretell loss of some description, possibly to do with the finances, but almost certainly of a material kind. This deficit might be due to a change in circumstances that's also to do with loss; loss of a job, a separation, a gamble that didn't pay off. It could also be due to simple over-spending.

However, sometimes it's necessary in our lives to undergo a process of "losing" things, to go back to zero and a fresh start. Although we wouldn't necessarily have wished these changes for ourselves, once the dust has settled and you can see where you are, there can come with the "loss" a profound sense of liberation. And if you

VI
Six of Coins

want to be philosophical about it, it's relatively easy to break it down "money" into what it really is; a simple token designed to be swapped for something else. Cowrie shells. There might be hard work ahead to regain your position, and there might need to be some sacrifices, but you will find eventually that you have gained far more than you lost.

Drawn Reversed

There's light at the end of the tunnel, and you know exactly what you need to do to be able to enjoy that brightness. You've been working hard in all areas to make up for lost ground, and you can feel the juggernaut starting to turn; events are now moving in your favor. You've had your head down for a while, but now there's a new sense of optimism and purpose, and you need to look around you and take care of those closest to you who may have been suffering during the process you've been undergoing. You might even think about taking a short break to restore the balance of your life which has been upset of late, due to other concerns.

KEYWORDS
Comfort; assistance; gifts

QUESTION INSPIRED BY THIS CARD:
WHAT IS THE TRUE NATURE OF GENEROSITY?

DRAWN UPRIGHT

There's a degree of karmic balance brought about by these six wrens; six is the number of union and balance, after all. Whatever is given freely reaps an equal reward at some point, and this might be what is happening in your life right now. It's important to remember there's generosity both in giving and receiving. Some people find it difficult to receive, but it's important to be able to receive graciously because this also allows the other person to be generous. This fact is frequently overlooked, but now is the time to be aware of it, be gracious, and to simply say "thank you." It's also possible that you're involved in some sort of a scheme which will give you the opportunity to be generous, either with your money, your time, or your talents. The benefits that will come to you will far outweigh anything that you bring to the equation, but this isn't the reason that you're doing it. You know what it is to struggle, you know how to extricate yourself from a mess, and you sincerely want to share these skills with others.

DRAWN REVERSED

There's a saying that a fool and his money are easily parted, and whilst you're certainly no fool, you are generous and giving and there are certain people who might want to take advantage of this. Be circumspect, if not wary, and carefully weigh up any financial schemes or "get rich quick" ideas that might be coming your way. If things seem too easy or simple then chances are that they are exactly that! There's also a possibility that there might be a financial shortfall somewhere that you hadn't anticipated which will need a degree of investigation to make sure that the fault doesn't lie elsewhere.

VII
SEVEN OF COINS

KEYWORDS
Harvest; reaping rewards; growth

QUESTION INSPIRED BY THIS CARD:
WHAT ARE MY PRIORITIES?

DRAWN UPRIGHT

It often takes a lot of hard work, keeping your head down, before you start to see the benefits of it. The seven wrens here are telling you that it's okay to look up now, and appreciate what you've managed to achieve. Imagine the analogy of a gardener who toils long and hard with the spade; the real pleasure is often in sitting down and doing nothing, simply enjoying the flowers! If you're not careful, you could get exhausted with the amount of work that you set yourself, and the intensity of your concentration means that you might even be having sleepless nights. So it's time to put some perspective in your life; your close friends and family would probably agree with this.

It might also be the case that a little streamlining might be in order, a cutting-away of any dead wood or parts of your life that have ceased to be either useful or beautiful. Again, it will require you to stand back for a moment to grasp which things need to go.

Drawn Reversed

You've been working hard for some time but it seems that you just can't see the wood for the trees. You feel unappreciated, and that your efforts are falling on stony ground. You might see others gaining promotions or salary increases whilst for some reason your own efforts go overlooked. All these factors can lead to you being unhappy in your work, and this dissatisfaction can take its toll in other aspects of your life, too. It might be time to take the bull by the horns and speak to your superiors, or you might also be thinking about taking a leap in the dark and going it on your own; there's a feeling here that you would like to be your own master for a change, and be totally in charge of your own destiny. Be careful to assess every aspect of your position before making a decision.

VIII
Eight of Coins

KEYWORDS
New learning; expansion; progress

QUESTION INSPIRED BY THIS CARD:
WHAT PROFITABLE ACTIVITY DO I MOST ENJOY?

DRAWN UPRIGHT

The eight wrens here are telling you that you have a time of education and expansion to look forward to. You might feel from time to time that you're being seriously stretched, but take courage that once you gain in confidence you will be more than worthy of the interesting challenges that face you. You'll also have the opportunity to apply the knowledge you've gained, and this could take the form of passing skills onto others. It's amazing just how much you realize you know when you're given the opportunity to teach others, and this too will be an empowering experience for you. As well as knowledge, you have made some diligent financial investments, too, and you'll be pleasantly surprised by the nest egg you've managed to put by.

Diligent progress is signified by this card, and you might feel from time to time that your pace is slightly more "plodding" than you're necessarily happy with. Stick with it; now is the time to be investing in the future, not simply in terms of finances but in terms of education and building for future generations.

DRAWN REVERSED

Reversed, the wrens bring with them a feeling of limitation or restriction. In some area of your life you might feel that you have expanded as far as is possible and that there's nowhere else for you to go. This leaves you feeling frustrated, and this frustration will spill into other areas of your life if you allow it to. As you see others making pace ahead of you, envy is added into the equation. In short, this is not a positive state of mind and you really need to make efforts to turn things around, by making sure that you're correct in your assumption that there's nowhere else to go, or by making practical changes in your life, or by altering your attitude, seeing what benefits there are to your situation and learning to be happy with your lot. This might mean looking for a new outlet that will give you the satisfaction you need.

IX
Nine of Coins

Keywords
Pleasure; enjoyment; prosperity

Question inspired by this card:
What more could I possibly want?

Drawn Upright

Here; the nine wrens tell you that you are willing and able to enjoy the benefits of your prosperity. You've worked hard and made wise investments. And after all, what are the finer things in life all about, if not to take pleasure in them? You deserve this. It's likely that you no longer need to work for a living, and you're rediscovering all the simpler things in life that are the pleasure of anyone, whether rich or poor; gardening, spending time with the family, cooking, enjoying the sunshine. Interests that you had to put to one side now come to the fore, and you might be thinking of taking up an old hobby or interest, or old friends that you haven't seen for a while may re-enter your life. There's also time for the pursuit of spiritual matters too, and you might decide to travel in order to expand these particular horizons.

Drawn Reversed

Here, the resources that you had taken for granted seem to be scarce. Maybe you've indulged too much in certain pleasures and now you have to be prepared to pay the price. Cut backs and "doing without" are signified by this card, but you will actually gain some satisfaction from chipping away at any debts that you might have incurred. It's also possible that you may have made some unwise investments. Where you thought there was going to be money, there's none, and you might have to think of additional ways of expanding your income. Take heart; nothing is insurmountable. You might decide to speak to an expert who will help you in these matters.

X
Ten of Coins

KEYWORDS
Family wealth; inheritance; a legacy

QUESTION INSPIRED BY THIS CARD:
WHAT DO I WANT TO LEAVE AS MY INHERITANCE?

DRAWN UPRIGHT

Counting your blessings is always a good idea, and the ten wrens here tell you that you have a lot of good things in your life. There's the notion with this card of leaving something for posterity, and that might take the form of a monetary legacy, or something else. You might be thinking about the wisest way to write a will in order that the family members will be satisfied, or you might yourself be the beneficiary of an inheritance of some kind. This card does tell of the inextricable links between family and money, and there may be a family business which you're concerned with. There are also responsibilities that come as a part of the equation, but again, this is to be welcomed. You're now able to reap the benefits of simply everything in your life, even the things that at the time seemed to be ill advised or of experiences what at the time seemed to be unhappy or unlucky; all have combined to make you the person that you now are, and this person is someone that you are objective enough to be happy about; no need for self-consciousness or false modesty! That you can "own" your own life in this way is a mark of just how blessed you truly are.

DRAWN REVERSED

These ten wrens, when drawn reversed, speak of family squabbles which are likely to be about money, or at least, wealth of some kind. It's easy to let such matters get out of proportion, but try to get some perspective. After all, the true wealth within a family is in the close, enduring relationships, and right now it's as well to remember that blood is thicker than water, and to try to calm things down before they go too far.

This card also signifies the draining of resources, whether this is to do with money, time, or simply energy. Be careful to make sure that you don't get overtired or overstretched.

XI
Queen of Coins

"I am no bird; and no net ensnares me; I am a free human being with an independent will."

~Charlotte Bronte

Keywords
Academic; diligent; shy

Description
The Queen of coins, a beautiful, seductively pouting woman with tumbling blonde hair, gazes provocatively back at us against a copper verdigris background. She wears a violet dress and a necklace bearing a symbol of the suit. There are three wrens with her; one in the foreground, one on a coin at the base of the card, and the third perches on her elbow.

Drawn Upright
Education, learning, and gathering wealth for the mind is what this Queen is all about. She stores up riches in the form of research and study, and the accumulation of knowledge. And this Queen therefore

has acquired the ability to draw conclusions and make new discoveries based on hard facts and this secure knowledge. A clever woman, more academically inclined rather than a heavyweight intellectual, the Queen of Coins is a pleasant, well-rounded person although possibly a little on the insecure or shy side, the type to forget what time it once they become wrapped up in work. In fact, it's easy for this person to let youth pass her by in the pursuit of learning, but at some point it will be time to apply all that education in the real world. Being able to do so will be a matter of gaining confidence; not the type to jump in at the deep end, people close to the Queen of Coins will be able to help her move forward by boosting her ego and reminding her of all her strong points. Sometimes inclined to be introverted and shy, the Queen can sometimes rely on alcohol or similar substances to help her navigate social situations.

DRAWN REVERSED

Introverted; works too hard; loss of money.

The studious nature of the Queen of Coins can sometimes mask a very introverted nature, and as a result she might find it difficult to make and retain any close relationships, driving her further into her work and as a result making her isolated. Knowing that this is a part of her nature can help, but until she gains a level of worldly experience she will need to be reminded at regular intervals that there's a big wide world out there; although books and learning are of great importance, it's also equally important to leave behind the theoretic world and embrace the experiential one! The Queen of Coins can also be afraid of expressing her feelings, since she has a fear of offending people, and is likely to put other peoples" emotional needs before her own. This means that she is apt to be the type to subsume her own emotional needs, which, if repressed for a long period of time, could manifest as an illness or allergy.

XII
The King of Coins

"The bird of paradise alights only upon the hand that does not grasp."
~John Berry

Keywords
Earthy; ambitious; determined

Description
The King of Coins looks back at us confidently, leaning against the background of copper verdigris. He wears quite an old-fashioned suit and tie with a purple cardigan. The symbol of the suit of coins peeps out from his top pocket, and he shares the painting with three wrens, one perched on each shoulder and one in the foreground. He looks relaxed, friendly, kind and approachable, but also has a shrewd expression on his face.

Drawn Upright
A man happy with his place in the world, the King of Coins is purposeful and determined, and has always had a sense that he knows where he is going, what he wants, and how to get it.

Sometimes we meet young children who are quite sure of what the future holds, and express, for example, an early desire to be a doctor. And then they go on to achieve it... This is the sort of quality displayed by this King. He is happy in the environment of this material world, a part of it, and able to use it to his own advantage in full cognizance of its nature. A sensualist, the King of Coins enjoys all the material pleasures the world has to offer, be they money, fine food and wine, belongings, and of course sex. Although this King is ambitious, his hard work and determination can make him something of a plodder, and some people might find him a little boring and obsessive. Spontaneity is a rare thing for him, and sometimes he needs people to "bring him out" of himself, to avoid the tunnel vision that could be an affliction. Practicality is all with the King of Coins; any kind of manual labor or getting his hands dirty will ultimately make him happy, and the end result a source of instant satisfaction.

Drawn Reversed

Obsessive; introspective; led only by material gain.

Because the King of Coins has a determined and stubborn ability to get his head down and work, work, work, he can lose the desire to socialize properly, and he may find that his life has become limited but doesn't know exactly what to do about it. He can find that he has retreated, by default, into an almost hermit-like existence. This is in itself not at all a bad thing, but requires a strength of mind and determination, combined with such an existence being born of a conscious decision, for this sort of a lifestyle to be really effective. It's not easy. If you have drawn this card and these factors don't relate to you, be aware that there might be someone in your circle who is in such a situation. If they do apply to you, then it may be time for you to make efforts to re-engage with the world; after all, amassing money is all very well, but you can't take it with you!

God and Goddess of Coins

The final royal pair in the Suit of Coins transform from wrens into magical, mystical owls. This switch is a reminder of the tale from the Mabinogion in which Bloduedd, the girl made from blossoms, is transformed into an owl. The delicate blue tracery on the wings of the owls is an homage to Alan Garner's extraordinary book, The Owl Service, which is a dark and imaginative reworking of the original tale.

XIII
The God of Coins

"No bird soars too high if he soars with his own wings."
~William Blake

Keywords
Wealth; industry; patience; sensuality; a gourmand.

Description
An older man, powerful, strong, the God of Coins embraces the bird which, for the purposes of this suit, switches from the wren to the owl in honor of the tale of Bloduedd, who, in the Mabinogion, was the beautiful woman that was constructed from flowers and was later turned into an owl. The God looks wealthy, plump, if tired; his eyes are closed.

Drawn Upright
This is the card of a Captain of Industry, someone who, through his own efforts, has enabled others to work, and has amassed wealth for himself and his family. This is the typical patriarch, maybe a self-made man, who loves the fact that he has provided security for others, and he loves to demonstrate this in practical terms by making sure that his home is a worthy showcase for his achievements. This God is discerning, cautious and shrewd, qualities necessary to his position and which he possessed even as a young man but which have been honed by necessity and experience; the result of this is that he can be quite an imposing figure on first meeting before he allows himself to relax. Being "on guard" is something that he has got used to. Although he can seem stern and as though he's a hard task-master, the King of Coins is a man of his word, full of integrity, and utterly reliable, a good and loyal friend.

His love of the good things in life means that he can sometimes overindulge and might sometimes need to be encouraged to rein in a little, or at least balance his life with exercise of some sort. Something of a traditionalist, this God can be disconcerted by the actions of some of his children, although any grandchildren would get away with murder!

Drawn Reversed

Stubborn; inflexible; mean; cruel.

The authority and control of the God of Coins can, if reversed, turn into a tyrannical bully who pays no attention to others. Those wonderful traditional values, allied to the kindliness and patience that's the usual trait of this God, can make him seem like a tedious old bore, and all the worst sorts of "traditional values" suddenly become his remit – misogyny and racism, for example, all the most heinous ideas of conservatism. Unfamiliarity, whether with people or a situation, can make him react badly, purely because he is nervous of being exposed, insecure in his own self despite the trappings of success which he uses as a barrier or control mechanism. Whereas he built his business on being open to possibilities, he now becomes closed off, opportunities pass him by, and his bitterness increases as he realizes this. This God now needs urgent help in order to help him back on the right path.

XIV
The Goddess of Coins

"Intelligence without ambition is a bird without wings."

~Salvador Dali

KEYWORDS
Warm, stable, practical, sensual.

DESCRIPTION
Against a copper verdigris background the Goddess of Coins stares provocatively back at us. Here, the wren has shape shifted magically into the owl, in homage to the fabulous tale from the Mabinogion of Bloduedd, the beautiful girl made of flowers who turns into an owl. The Goddess is calm, confident, beautiful, the roses in her hair matching the roses on her dress.

DRAWN UPRIGHT
This is a beautiful, elegant and warm woman, her feet firmly in the material world, and a lover of all the sensual delights. She has money, and will spend it on the most beautiful things she can find, has an eye for a bargain but will also think nothing of spending a large amount of cash on something that she simply has to have. She loves preparing food for lots of people, throwing parties, entertaining her guests lavishly and with exquisite attention to detail. She loves art, and is fascinated by artists and writers, sculptors; she is likely to count such people amongst those guests. She is also fond of animals and will occasionally have one or two strays running around, which may or may not be rehoused at some point.

The Goddess of Coins makes a wonderful friend. In any kind of crisis, she will roll her sleeves up and get involved. She treats her close friends as family members, always with open arms and an open heart. Her home environment is of paramount importance, and she always has an open house and many people coming and going, attracted to her generosity and warmth. Strangers, captivated by her charm, soon become friends.

In matters of the heart, this Goddess will sometimes struggle to find an equal, since most men will not have the necessary god-like qualities that she needs to be able to expand and shine for herself. She is sensuous and giving, a wonderful partner in any kind of joint business endeavors.

Drawn Reversed

Selfish; calculating; over-indulgent; takes advantage of others.

All the wonderful qualities of this Goddess, when reversed, start to look mean. Worried about her own generosity, she will cut off suddenly if she feels that someone has taken advantage of her; this can reflect unfairly on other friends, and if she's feeling insecure she might react in ways contrary to her true nature; she will start to place money over friendships, preferring to work long hours to amass wealth, but will become miserly, seeing the money as a means to an end. The very worst aspect of this is that she may stay tied to an unhappy relationship for the sake of the material wealth and benefits that it might bring.

Her ambition is such that she will always make a success in her chosen field; drawn reversed, however, warns that she might lose friends in the process.

Divination with the Secret Language of Birds Tarot

Any deck of Tarot cards is, effectively, a sacred object; the images and symbols contained within the 78 cards are a rich storybook, the stuff of dreams and the imagination. When you hold a Tarot deck in your hands you're a living part of their long, long history, and you're also a part of a significant magical inheritance.

But how should these mystical cards be used? This largely depends on your own preference, and for all the "rules" you might come across, it really is completely up to you. You might have a very formal approach, or you might prefer your readings to be more relaxed. So long as you're comfortable, it really doesn't matter.

Pictures speak so much louder than words, and there's a school of thought that says you should simply ignore any text and just look at the cards and say out loud what springs to mind. Indeed, this can be a very effective way of reading the Tarot, especially if you're psychically gifted.

But bear in mind that the cards don't have to be used to do intuitive readings for other people. Lots of people just pull a card from the deck occasionally to see what guidance and insight the images offer. This is actually a very good way of becoming familiar with the cards, too, as well as being fun.

Tarot Card Superstitions

There are a lot of superstitions about Tarot cards, but for the most part, these can be largely ignored since they don't seem to make a whole lot of logical sense. For instance, some people say you should always sleep with the deck under your pillow; others say the opposite, that to do so will give you bad dreams.

Lets' choose some of the more prevalent superstitions about these cards and see if there's any credence in them.

* **You should never buy your own deck.**
This particular superstition, if obeyed, would rule out the many serious Tarot collectors out there. Cards are not always bought just for use; they are often bought for their artistic merit and imaginative interpretations. In addition, many readers, both professional and amateur, generally buy their own decks. It's true that an interest in the Tarot might stem from a first deck being presented as a gift, but beyond that, this particular belief just doesn't make sense. It might stem from a belief that money shouldn't change hands for a deck, but again this would render obsolete the stores that sell Tarot and publishers that publish them!

* **Tarot cards should be stored in a silk bag.**
Silk is meant to protect from negative influences. It's true that careful storage of a sacred object helps us to regard that object as such, but again, the use of silk as a way of somehow "protecting" the cards really isn't necessary and is really up to the owner.

* **Tarot decks should be handled only by their owner.**
Again, how would Tarot readers operate if this were the case, given that the cards need to be shuffled by the querant?

* **Tarot cards should be stored in a high place when not being used.**
A high place is, symbolically, the origin of inspiration from the skies. So while we can see the reasoning behind this superstition, again, it's not necessary.

* **Perhaps the biggest superstition of all is that there are "bad" cards.**
The Devil and the Hanging Man, in particular, are singled out in this way. But any discerning reader knows that there's no such thing as a "bad" card or a "bad" card reading. (That's not to say that there are no "bad" card readers out there!) Life is full of ups and downs, and the images on the tarot reflect this beautifully. After all, learning to cope with everything that life throws at us is what this journey is all about.

SPREADS

Learning a few different spreads is the key to all tarot readings. You might want to experiment with different types until you find one that you're comfortable with, and you can find extensive books on the subject. You might also want to invent your own method of laying out the cards

There are three methods of spreading the cards included here; one traditional (the Celtic Cross), one less well known (the Wheel or Migration) and one that has been designed specifically with *The Secret Language of Birds Tarot* in mind; this spread is called Flock.

But before the cards are spread, they need to be shuffled.

The questioner should sit across the table from the reader, and both should be in as calm and meditative a state as possible. The lead in this should be taken by the reader, who will invite the questioner to concentrate on his or her problem or question whilst shuffling the cards in any way, and for as long as he or she prefers. Then some readers ask for the cards to be cut as many times as the Questioner cares to do it, and for the cut deck to be put back together again. Then, the reading...

The Celtic Cross

This spread appears in just about every Tarot book going, and it is a very popular spread, so it seemed right to include it here too.

After shuffling, the cards are taken one at a time and laid in the way shown in the diagram.

The cards are read as follows.

1. The factors that bring you to the current situation.
2. The key influence that is the cause of this situation.
3. The influences of past experiences and events.
4. The influence of new experiences and experiences.
5. This card is about the opposition of negative and positive forces and gives guidance as to a course of action.
6. The influences of the near future.
7. This card indicates whether your actions are the correct ones given the circumstances.
8. Surprise elements and random events
9. How you might adapt in the future
10. Culmination. This card summarizes the entire reading and does not necessarily involve any future projections.

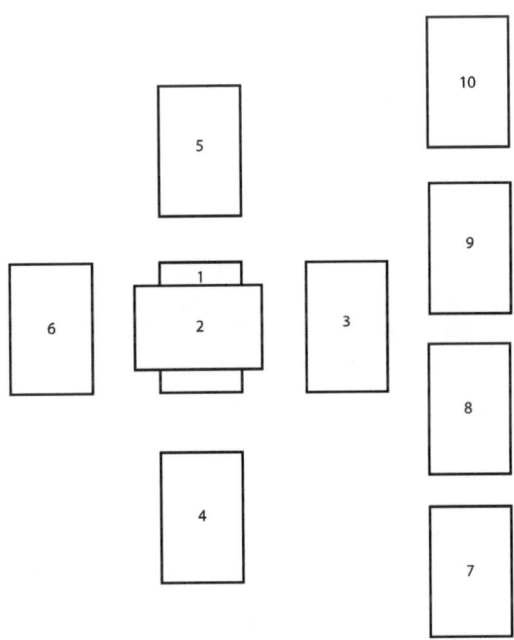

The Wheel

The next spread is called the Wheel, or the Circle or, for the purposes of this Tarot, the Migration, since it represents the flight of birds around the globe.

After shuffling the cards are laid out in the order shown.

The interpretation is as follows.

1. How you see yourself.
2. How others see you.
3. How you communicate.
4. The home and immediate surroundings.
5. Enjoyable events – leisure time, close relationships, etc.
6. The working life.
7. Relationships with a practical aspect.
8. The cycle of life and what's happening right now.
9. What lies ahead.
10. What you would like to achieve; unfulfilled dreams and ambitions.
11. How to make these dreams come true.
12. The aspect that is currently obstructing these dreams.
13. Culmination; this final card summarizes the whole spread.

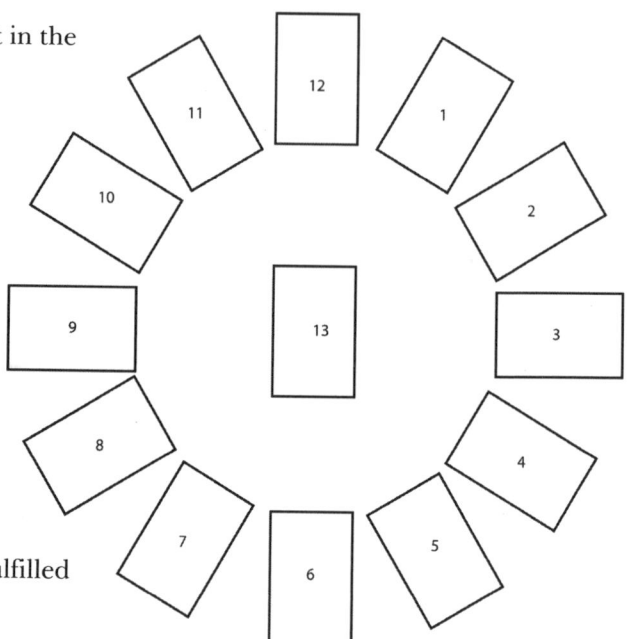

The Flock

The final spread show here is called Flock, and takes on the shape of a flock of birds.

Laying out the cards in the sequence shown, here are the meanings.

1. Your current situation
2. The immediate influence
3. A past influence
4. A future influence
5. The block
6. The source of help
7. Culmination or summing-up

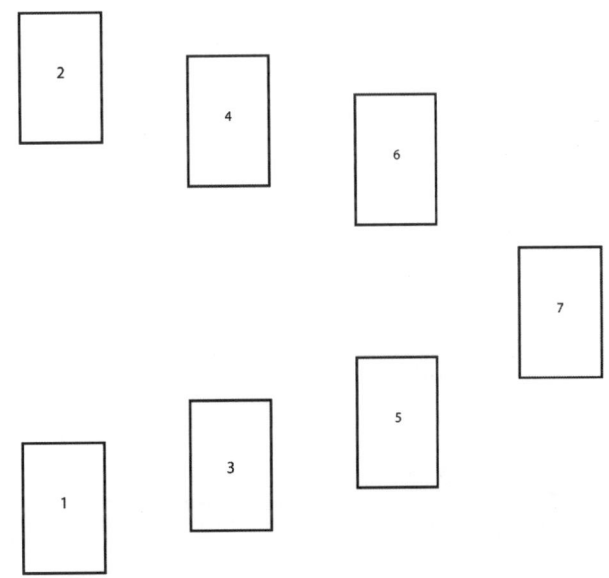

NOTES ON REVERSALS

Generally speaking, a reversed card signifies the opposing values which are described as "keywords." However, "opposing" is often confused with "negative," and there is certainly nothing negative about a reversed card. It's great to know our strengths and give ourselves a pat on the back for them, but knowing our weaknesses is actually far more constructive, because then we have a chance to improve ourselves and the lot that life has given us. The Tarot, as life, is about finding harmony and balance between opposing forces, and the reversed card is a healthy reminder of this ideal.

Conclusion

We hope that you enjoy using this deck, and that its images inspire you to access the place where time does not exist, and where past, present, and future meld together in a seamless infinity. This is the Otherworld that those ancient Augurs sought to find, losing themselves in the flight patterns and behavior of the wild birds that surrounded them.

You don't necessarily need a tarot deck to find this alternate Universe. Next time you are outdoors, try watching the real birds.

Respect them.

Understand them.

Meditate on them.

Extend your senses; stretch to meet the Infinite and realize that you are a part of it. See where the birds take you.

Enjoy your flight.